Q&A

Questions and Answers on

Freshwater Aquarium Fishes

Q&A

Questions and Answers on

Freshwater Aquarium Fishes

Dr. Ashley Ward

tfh

PUBLISHED BY
TFH Publications, Inc.
One TFH Plaza
Third and Union Avenues
Neptune City, NJ 07753

ISBN 978-0-7938-0621-8

This book has been published with
the intent to provide accurate and
authoritative information in regard
to the subject matter within. While
every reasonable precaution has been
taken in preparation of this book, the
author and publisher expressly disclaim
responsibility for any errors, omissions,
or adverse effects arising from the use
of the information contained herein. The
techniques and suggestions are used at
the reader's discretion and are not to be
considered a substitute for veterinary
care. If you suspect a medical problem,
consult a veterinarian.

CREDITS
Created and compiled: Ideas into Print,
Claydon, Suffolk, England

Design and prepress: Stuart Watkinson,
Ayelands, Longfield, Kent, England

Computer graphics: Stuart Watkinson

Production management: Consortium,
Poslingford, Suffolk, England

Print production: Sino Publishing House
Ltd., Hong Kong

Printed and bound in China
07 08 09 10 11 1 3 5 7 9 8 6 4 2

Author

Dr. Ashley Ward, BSc is a Visiting Research Fellow at the Institute of Integrative and
Comparative Biology at Leeds University. He is a fish biologist, currently based at the
University of Sydney in Australia, where he conducts research into the behavior of fishes.
During his career, he has looked at a whole range of different aspects of fish behavior,
including fish intelligence, feeding, and schooling behavior and the breeding behavior of
cichlids. As well as studying fish in the aquarium, Dr. Ward takes every opportunity to get
out into the wild to study fish in their natural environment.

Library of Congress Cataloging-in-Publication Data
Ward, Ashley.
  Questions and answers on freshwater aquariums fishes : everything you
need to know to successfully raise healthy fish / Ashley Ward.
      p. cm.
  Includes index.
  ISBN 978-0-7938-0621-8 (alk. paper)
  1. Aquariums--Miscellanea. 2. Aquarium fishes--Miscellanea. I.
Title.
  SF457.3.W37 2007
  639.34--dc22
                                    2007017835

Below: Rainbowfishes from Australia are peaceful aquarium fish.

Freshwater Aquarium Fishes

Contents

Freshwater Aquarium Fishes

Introduction

The activity and the dramatic swirling colors of tropical fish may be what initially draws most newcomers to the fishkeeping hobby, but once the home aquarium and its inhabitants are established then it is very often the fishes' behavior patterns that intrigue. Watching the fish can often provoke questions in the minds of their owners, such as "Why is my fish behaving like this?" or "How does it do that?" Understanding the "hows" and "whys" of fish behavior brings a whole new dimension to the hobby and in this book, I will take a comprehensive look at all the fascinating elements of fish behavior and explain these "hows" and "whys" for each.

Left: Good fishkeepers understand how their fish behave.

Chapter 1
Fish in their world

Fish are among the most diverse of all animals. They are found in a huge variety of shapes, sizes, and colors, each perfectly fitted to the role they fill within their habitat, enabling them not only to survive, but to prosper.

The way in which all animals, including fish, perceive their environment is through their sensory system. Their senses – vision, olfaction (smell), gustation (taste), and pressure detection – are shaped by the world in which they live and produce an impression of their surroundings.

Below: The serpae tetras (Hyphessobrycon eques) *have excellent eyesight and a well-developed sense of smell.*

Q: How are fish adapted to their environment?

A: Fish are one of the most successful groups of animals on the planet. There are over 25,000 species of fish occupying every imaginable habitat, from inhospitable, sulphurous thermal springs to temporary pools in the tropics that fill and dry up on an annual cycle. In each case, the fish are adapted to meet the demands of their habitat. For example, a fish living in the turbid, muddy waters so typical of many South American and African rivers may rely less on vision than on its other senses, such as smell and taste. In fact, some species living in these conditions, such as the mormyrids, or elephant-nosed fishes, use electroreception – a kind of inbuilt radar system – to find their prey and to interact with others.

Q: How do fish use the information they gather?

A: Like all animals, fish are continually gathering information about their environment. This information is received and decoded by the fish's brain, which then transmits a response. So if a nocturnal predator approaches under cover of darkness, any surrounding prey fish may detect a large pressure wave using their lateral line. This information will be transmitted to the brain via the spinal column. In response, the

Above: *A school of penguin tetras* (Thayeria boehlkei) *have detected food and are streaming towards it.*

brain will then stimulate muscles to contract to cause the fish to swim away from the direction of the pressure wave and therefore the predator that produced it. At the same time, the fish may gather other information about the predator – it may smell it, for instance, or hear if any small stones are displaced by it as it moves from concealment.

Although the fish's brain receives all this information, the fish does not have to "think" about swimming away; the movement away from the predator is a simple response.

Q: *What gets a fish's attention?*

A: Certain stimuli may gain the attention of a fish more quickly than others, so a small animal swimming actively through the water column might attract the attentions of a hungry fish more than if it hid in the substrate. Similarly, a faint smell of food may cause a fish to try to orientate itself towards the source of the smell, whereas once it closes in on the smell, the signal becomes stronger and stimulates the fish to switch into an intense feeding state. At this point it may be far less able to react to other signals. For this reason, the predators of guppies often time their attacks to when their prey has itself found food.

Fish in lake habitats

Freshwater fish live in an amazing variety of habitats. Evolution has shaped both their appearance and their senses over countless generations and millions of years to produce the most effective adaptations to fit the conditions in which they live.

Q: *What is it like living in a lake?*

A: The still, clear waters of lakes provide an ideal habitat for fish. Free from any extreme fluctuations in temperature or water chemistry, these stable bodies of water are often home to teeming communities of fish. Nowhere provides a better example of this than the lakes of the Rift Valley in East Africa – the cichlids of Lake Malawi and Lake Tanganyika in particular are well known to aquarists. The waters of these lakes are brightly lit by the equatorial sun and are rich in food; both the algae and the invertebrates that the cichlids depend on are abundant. Both Malawi and Tanganyika are huge lakes and their isolation has produced in each a species flock that is endemic to its own lake – it has been estimated that Lake

Malawi alone is home to around 450 species of cichlids. Almost all of these live in the clear, oxygen-rich waters of the shallows and most live among the complex, rocky substrate at the water's edge, which provides both a nursery for the young and the territories of the adults.

Q: *How are fish adapted for living in lakes?*

A: The African Rift Lakes are full of different habitats for fishes. Many species imported for the aquarium hobby are mbuna, which live along the rocky parts of the lake's shore. A long, thin

Above: The rocky shores of Mumbo Island in Lake Malawi are home to countless fishes.

Right: Crystal-clear water conditions such as this are the norm for much of the year in Lake Malawi.

*The vivid colors of
Tropheus moorii
are excellent for
communicating in
the clear water
lake habitat.*

Q: Which senses do Rift Lake cichlids use most?

A: Light penetrates deep into the clear waters of the lakes so the cichlids' habitat is brightly lit. Under these conditions, vision is extremely important and this is reflected in the large eyes common to many of these fish. The brilliant colors of the cichlids, including vivid yellows and electric blues, and the dramatic patterns seen in many of the Tanganyikan cichlids, are also features of brightly lit environments because the fish use bold visual signals between one another. Nevertheless, the fish also use smell to back this up, especially when it comes to searching out hidden prey and assessing potential mates.

body shape is ideal in this habitat as it allows the fish to maneuver around the rocks and into crannies and caves. Many fish that live in a current use their tail fins to propel themselves. However, Rift Lake cichlids often rely on their pectoral fins for this, which allows them to maneuver with pinpoint accuracy and, unusually for freshwater fish, it also allows them to swim backwards – ideal for investigating and then backing out of tight rocky crevices. Other Rift cichlid species, such as *Nimbochromis livingstonii* and *Protomelas taeniolatus*, are found in the sandy bays or open water of these inland seas. These species have deeper bodies than the mbuna, which are necessary for rotating the fishes in open water, or when feeding at the substrate. They also use a greater degree of tail-propulsion for their swimming.

*A long, thin body, such
as that of* Labeotropheus
trewavasae, *is perfect for
maneuvering in a rocky
environment.*

*The mottled colors
of* Nimbochromis
livingstonii *help
to conceal it from
predators and
prey alike.*

Fish in river habitats

Most of the familiar fish kept by aquarists, from tetras to rasboras and from angelfish to many of the well-known catfish, are native to rivers across the tropics. Some of these rivers are huge – the Amazon river alone holds within its banks an incredible 20% of all the world's freshwater. The character of a river typically changes as it flows from its hilly origins to the wide, mature stretches that wind across the country to the sea. A river can also change throughout the year, flooding during the rains but slowing to a trickle during the dry season. River fishes, therefore, have to cope with a wide variety of conditions. The benefit to the aquarist is that they tend to be less demanding about their conditions in an aquarium.

Below: Some fish, such as this river loach Sewellia lineolata, *use specially adapted fins to prevent themselves from being swept away.*

Q: *What are the characteristics of fish that live in fast-flowing rivers?*

A: In the upper reaches the river is fast-flowing and well-oxygenated, but this is a hostile environment for fish. Few can withstand the current and even for those that can, there is little food. Nonetheless, some fish do make their home here among the rapids, including the White Cloud Mountain minnows; the blockhead cichlid *(Steatocranus)*, which seeks refuge and hunts among the boulders of the rivers of West

Above: White Cloud Mountain minnows (Tanichthys albonubes) *have a typically streamlined shape for life in flowing water.*

Africa; and the *Plecostomus* catfish, which grazes on the film of algae covering the substrate, holding itself in the current with its powerful sucking mouth. Living in this harsh environment demands adaptations – most importantly a streamlined body shape. The noise of the tumbling waters and the turbulence mean that detecting pressure or faint odors in the water is difficult. At close quarters food may be sniffed out, but vision is of primary importance in these clear waters.

Q: *How do things change for fish as the river currents slow?*

A: As the river moves downstream, the pace relents and life for fish is easier. Often, pools form along the course

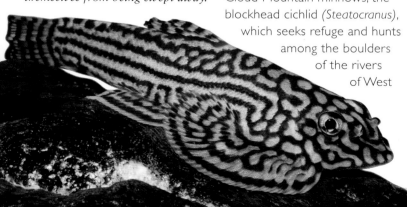

Q: What kinds of fish live in the lower reaches?

A: When the river reaches lowland plains, it widens and slows to a leisurely pace. In many of the larger rivers of the tropics, the water is colored by tannins and organic debris. The deeper waters allow little light to penetrate and the catfish that live along the bottom rely heavily on smell and taste to find food and to recognize others. The silty substrate harbors a rich array of invertebrates, and species such as the elephant-nosed fish probe for them in the darkness. Nearer the surface and at the margins, fish such as cardinal tetras use their brilliant livery to signal to one another and keep to their schools.

Above: The waters of the Rio Usumacinta, which flows along the borders of Mexico and Guatemala, are home to a host of cichlids, catfishes and tetras.

of the river, offering a current-free haven for many species. Many of the familiar Central American cichlids occupy these reaches, breeding among the stones of the river bed, often in the larger pools out of the current. Here, streamlining is less important but even so, fish such as guppies occupy the water margins to avoid both the currents and the threat of predation. For most of the year the water is clear, allowing the fish to hunt and identify other fish by sight. As the water slows, chemical cues become ever more important. Body

shape is more variable than in the upper reaches. Deep bodies allow maneuverability out of the current, whereas more torpedo-shaped profiles are common among those fish that live in the water current.

Powerful muscles and streamlining are essential for river fish.

Right: The blockhead cichlid (Steatocranus casuarius) *is perfectly at home in the rivers of the Congo.*

Fish in marshes and ditches

Many of the fish that find their way into aquariums originate from harsh, inhospitable habitats. Some of the conditions found in aquatic habitats in Southeast Asia are among the most difficult. Constrained into receding marshes and ditches for most of the year, the onset of the rains expands their environment across shallow paddy fields and low-lying fields. Such habitats are often choked with vegetation and low in oxygen, making life a constant struggle against these hostile conditions.

Q: *What is life like in the long dry season?*

A: For much of the year, during the long dry season, fish may be trapped in isolated areas of habitat in ditches and ponds of stagnant water. Often, populations of fish become concentrated by the receding waters, so competition for space, for food, and for the limited oxygen is intense. On top of this, the large numbers of fish attract the attentions of predators, such as wading birds. Plants also invade the water with their roots

Above: The swamps and paddy fields of Asia provide a rich habitat for many aquarium fishes, including many gouramis, catfish, loaches, barbs, and rasboras.

and stems, covering the surface with their leaves. Open water habitat is therefore at a premium and light is restricted.

Q: *What adaptations do fish show to these habitats?*

A: Despite the tough conditions, fish not only survive but seem to thrive. The secret of the fishes' success lies in their adaptations. Perhaps the most dramatic of these is the ability

---

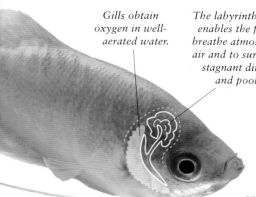

Gills obtain oxygen in well-aerated water.

The labyrinth organ enables the fish to breathe atmospheric air and to survive in stagnant ditches and pools.

Above: *The croaking gourami (Trichopsis vittatus) uses sound to communicate in the turbid waters.*

of some species, including the Anabantoids – the gouramis and their relatives – to breathe atmospheric oxygen using the remarkable labyrinth organ. This adaptation allows the fish to live in some of the most difficult conditions, occupying habitats where the lack of dissolved oxygen excludes others. Size also matters in these conditions; a large body is a disadvantage in the tangled, airless conditions, so the fish that live in them are usually small. Maneuvering in the thick vegetation and the bottom mud to find the prey that live there requires a flexible body, and no fish exemplifies this more than the kuhli loach, which lives in these waters.

Q: *What happens when the rain arrives?*

A: The influx of water that comes with the rains expands the fishes' habitat across a wide range of low-lying land, including the fields of rice that thrive under these conditions. The shallow waters are rich in food and after the daily struggle during the dry season, fish can now grow and breed. Although the rains expand the habitat, the water remains extremely turbid – visibility may never increase above a few inches – so just as in the blackwater regions of the Amazon, fish must rely on their other senses. Smell and taste are especially important for these fish. The barbels of loaches, for example, are covered in sensory cells to detect small prey, such as snails and worms, in the soft mud. Croaking gouramis communicate extensively with sound, while other gouramis use specially adapted pectoral fins to feel their way around their world, in much the same way as insects use their antennae.

Left: *The body plan of the kuhli loach* (Pangio kuhlii) *is perfect for exploring cluttered, muddy habitats.*

Life on the edge

Aquatic habitats are among the most varied anywhere on the planet. Conditions can be extreme and changeable over short periods of time. The fish that live in these environments must adapt to succeed. This remarkable ability means that fish are able to exploit habitats that are beyond the capabilities of other species. It allows these pioneers to prosper, away from the competition of others.

Q: *What are the hardships of living in an estuary?*

A: Life in the world's estuaries is one of constant change. Every six hours, as the tides ebb and flow, the water chemistry undergoes a complete transformation from salt to freshwater and vice versa. The physiological demands on creatures in this habitat are extreme, but for those that are able to adapt, there are rich food resources to exploit, such as are found in mangrove swamps. Few species are able to cope with the stresses of living in estuaries, meaning that those who can have fewer competitors.

Q: *Can fish survive in temporary pools?*

A: The short rainy season experienced in parts of equatorial Africa produces temporary pools that dry up to no more than cracked mud and dust once the rains recede. Yet even under these conditions,

some fish still manage to eke out a living. Many species of killifish hatch, grow and reproduce during an incredibly short period of time. Turquoise killifish (*Nothobranchius furzeri*) typically complete their life cycle in just ten weeks. Shortly after the arrival of the rains, the eggs hatch, producing tiny larvae that

The sheltering lungfish

As water levels drop, lungfish seek shelter in the thick layer of mud at the bottom of their pool, where they can remain for months.

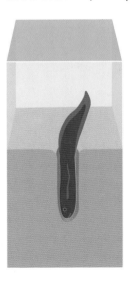

A narrow connection to the surface prevents the lungfish from suffocating.

1 *Buried in mud, the fish is protected from drying out when the water evaporates.*

2 *Within the damp mud, the lungfish is safe from the effects of the glaring sun.*

3 *As the mud dries out, the lungfish secretes a cocoon to hold in moisture.*

Above: Mangrove swamps are a feature of tropical coasts. The mangrove's roots provide a haven for young fish.

Below: The mangrove killi (Kryptolebias marmoratus) can survive for extended periods out of water.

feed on algal cells and other newly hatched aquatic creatures. Growth is extremely rapid, the fish attaining full size after only a few weeks. During this time they mature sexually and begin to reproduce before the pools disappear under the hot sun. But as the adults die, the eggs remain in a state of suspended animation. Unlike the eggs of other fish species, killifish eggs are protected by a shell consisting of several layers, and remain viable until the rains return months later. But not all fish that live in such conditions die once the waters vanish. Lungfish burrow into the soft mud and estivate – a state of being akin to the hibernation of many mammals that live in temperate climates. The body's metabolic processes

slow to a minimum and the animal awaits better conditions, which in the case of the lungfish, means the return of the rains.

Q: Can fish leave the water?

A: Some fish species take a different approach to this seasonal loss of habitat. When

temporary pools disappear or become too harsh to support life, some species leave the pools to cross land in search of new habitats. Some, such as the mangrove killifish (*Kryptolebias marmoratus*) move regularly between tiny water bodies and are able to survive extended periods out of water in damp leaf litter. Others, such as the climbing perch and *Clarias* catfish, are able to travel considerable distances in their search for a new home. Mudskippers, which live in estuarine conditions across Australasia, are equally happy in water or on the shoreline, where the males construct nests out of the water. In fact, these unusual fish spend more time out of water than in, climbing over roots and dashing across mudflats.

Below: Mudskippers carry a supply of water within their gills, enabling them to breathe when on land.

Communicating through color

The diversity and brilliance of the colors of tropical fish are responsible in part for their popularity in the home aquarium. In the wild, these colors act as signals between fish, signifying anything from sexiness to anger and from fear to health. Colors may change over the course of a fish's life but, to make sure each individual fish within a species is "speaking" the same color "language," the signal each color pattern conveys remains the same.

As the oscar cichlid (Astronotus ocellatus) calmly patrols its territory, its color pattern is normal.

Just moments later, its attention is engaged by a rival and its colors rapidly intensify.

Q: *Can color reflect a fish's state of health?*

A: Fish color patterns are seldom fixed. Instead, they vary throughout the fish's lifetime and even day to day. When a fish looks "washed out" or drab in comparison to its normal appearance this can often indicate that it is ill or stressed. If steps are taken to address the root cause, the fish will eventually regain its former glory. Bright and well-defined colors show that the fish is in top condition. The aquarist can promote this by paying attention to diet and water chemistry, providing the correct pH and hardness, and keeping nitrates to an absolute minimum with good filtration.

Q: *Do fish change their color with their "mood"?*

A: Yes, fish are able to communicate their mood through color. Following a bout of aggression between oscar cichlids, a losing fish will often signal its submission by darkening its color patterns. This may be a signal in its own right or it may simply help the loser blend into the background, making the aggressor less likely to follow up with another attack. A study on *Tilapia* revealed 14 distinct color patterns relating to fish mood, each communicating a subtly different message to other fish, ranging from aggression to arousal, and from fright to territoriality.

Q&A

Q: *Why are young fis often a different color to mature ones?*

A: As fish grow and mature, their color patterns may change. Juveniles tend to adopt comparatively drab colors, only to bloom as adults. This is because, in the wild, a small, brightly colored fish is unlikely to survive to adulthood – vivid colors attract predators. However, when the fish reaches maturity, it needs to advertise to potential mates, so it begins to invest in dazzling colors.

Q: *How do fish create and change their color?*

A: The colors a fish displays are governed by "chromatophores" – cells that cover the animal and contain color pigments. There are several different types of chromatophores, each responsible for a different element of fish coloration. Perhaps the most important of these are the melanophores, which contain the black pigment melanin and which affect the darkness of, for instance, a banding pattern. Melanophores, especially, are capable of rapid change in response to the fish's mood or to the environment. If these cells distribute the pigment

How fish change color

The skin of fish contains pigment cells that overlap one another and change in response to the fish's mood to alter the way it looks.

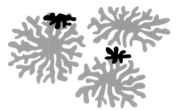

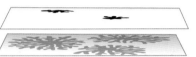

The melanophores are activated, producing a bold dark pattern on the fish's flanks.

Now the yellow/red pigment in the erythrophores has spread out and the dark pigment has retracted.

evenly across themselves, the fish appears dark, but if the pigment is gathered up into clumps, it appears lighter. Other chromatophores contain other pigments and are responsible for different colors. These include the erythrophores, which hold carotenoids and affect the levels

of yellow to red coloration. Iridophores contain guanine and are responsible for both the silvery shimmer of fish such as tinfoil barbs and, because of the way the guanine crystals reflect light, iridescent colors such as the blue stripe of a neon tetra.

Right: When tinfoil barbs (Barbonymus schwanenfeldii) are in top condition, they have silvery metallic flanks and bold red fins.

Communicating through behavior

Body language and behavioral cues are vital for communication between all visual animals, and fish are no exception. A wide variety of signals can be transmitted through body language, some are relatively subtle but others are very deliberate and obvious; when it is important to get your message across it is best not to leave any room for ambivalence.

▌ *Two rival green terrors ("Aequidens" rivulatus) come face to face, each studying the other's behavior to work out its intentions.*

Q: *What do fish use body language for?*

A: Much of the body language of fish is devoted to defending their own interests. When two neon tetras squabble, they display to one another, each rigidly holding out its fins to show the other that it is both large and in great shape. This flank display is sometimes augmented by spreading the gill covers, again to impress the rival with size (see page 140). Fish are usually very exaggerated and stereotypical in their aggressive displays; some enact a very rigid, almost robotic, slow swimming pattern, making absolutely sure they can be seen by a rival. Although there are similarities between species,

individuals within the same species tend to use virtually identical body language to make sure that everyone is "speaking the same language." This can be quite bizarre – some species of goby adopt a display posture with their head raised and their mouth gaping open.

Q: *How do fish communicate fright or submission?*

A: As well as informing the world at large that you are prepared to fight your corner, there are also times when dangerous aggressors have to be appeased. Perhaps not surprisingly, one of the best ways to do this is to adopt a posture that is the opposite of the usual threat display. A defensive fish will therefore often fold its fins and

do everything it can to convince the aggressor that it poses no danger, including swimming with its head up and backing off. This latter is the most important element in communicating submission and is one reason why aggression in the aquarium can sometimes continue to the death – a fish in the aquarium can obviously only back off so far, so the aquarist needs to look out for the signals in order to separate fish before it comes to this.

Q: *Do fish use body language for courtship?*

A: Female fish tend to be choosy, so males of many species have to work hard to impress their potential mates. One of the ways that males can achieve this is by displaying, helping the

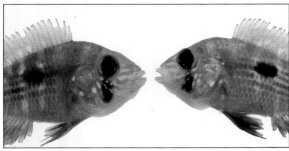

2 *Closing in, the two fish continue to communicate through signals, such as rigid fins and slow, almost awkward swimming.*

3 *At close quarters, the visual signals are stepped up through the use of a typical aggression signal – flared gill covers.*

female to decide if he will make a good father. Female guppies are harassed almost continuously by males, both in the aquarium and in the streams of their home in Trinidad. To avoid this, the females move into deeper, faster-flowing water where the smaller males find it hard to follow, even risking predation to rid themselves of the incessant attentions of the males. If a male is to mate successfully, he can invest in a display, which, if it impresses, will allow him the chance to mate successfully without the female darting off. Males that build nests need to advertise the presence of their constructions

4 *Once the flared gill covers are backed up with an open-mouthed display then more direct aggression is usually not far off.*

5 *Jaw locking enables the fish to test each other's strength before a full-scale fight.*

to females. The proud owner will patrol an area around his nest, intercepting any females that swim past. The male can then use a wide variety of displays to tempt the female back to his nest. Each species has its own display – for instance,

male sticklebacks swim in an exaggerated zigzag to attract the attentions of their mates.

Chemical messages underwater

Fish detect the chemical cues that surround them using both their senses of smell (olfaction) and taste (gustation). Of these two, olfaction is considered the most important, especially over long distances. Fish use taste to assess things that are physically in contact with the taste cells. The underwater environment is a soup, full of chemical messages. Fish constantly intercept these messages, using their highly developed sense of smell, choosing which to respond to and which to ignore.

Many active predators, such as this piranha (Pygocentrus nattereri) have prominent nostrils that help to detect prey.

The nostril's structure draws in water.

Tiny chemical traces are present in water.

Water circulates through the nostril.

Chemical traces are detected by sensory cells.

Q: *Do fish have noses?*

A: Not exactly – but they can smell. Unlike many land animals, fish do not breathe through their nostrils; these are used instead solely for smell. Some species have two pairs of nostrils and actively pump water in through one pair and out through the other, so that the water passes over the sensory receptors responsible for detecting the chemical messages. They

may then be decoded by the olfactory bulbs, which sit in the forebrain of the fish.

Q: *How well can fish smell?*

A: A good sense of smell is essential for many species of fish because vision can often be limited underwater by turbid, muddy water and shade from plants, such as lilies. The ability

of fish to detect chemicals varies, but is strongest in those species that live with the least light. Fish in the deep seas are able to detect concentrations of chemicals as weak as one part per quadrillion – put into understandable terms, this is about the same as being sensitive enough to detect a balloon in North America. Although this is an extreme case, an excellent sense of smell is common to

many species of fish. The ability of blind cave fish to compete successfully for food in a tank containing sighted competitors is a case in point. Although the cave fish cannot track the food visually, its excellent sense of smell means that it is able to build up a chemical profile of its habitat and use this to locate a meal.

Q: *How do fish use smell?*

A: The ability of fish to orientate towards (or away from) the source of an odor is called chemotaxis. Each animal produces its own odor; if a fish detects the odor of a prey animal, it is likely to try to use this to track down that animal. The process of discovering the source of a smell starts when the fish, in this case, crosses the odor trail of the prey animal. Once the fish detects the presence of the smell, it circles to reconnect with the trail and then moves up the odor gradient, going from a weak smell to a stronger one, until it finds the source and devours it. As well as finding food, fish are able to navigate using their sense of smell. The most famous of all fish species for doing this are salmon, but most fish are capable of detecting and moving towards the smell of a local, familiar habitat. Each habitat has a unique chemical signature and it is this that the fish respond to. This ability is extremely important – fish that become familiar with a preferred area of their habitat know from experience where the best hiding places are and where food can be found.

Homing in on the prey

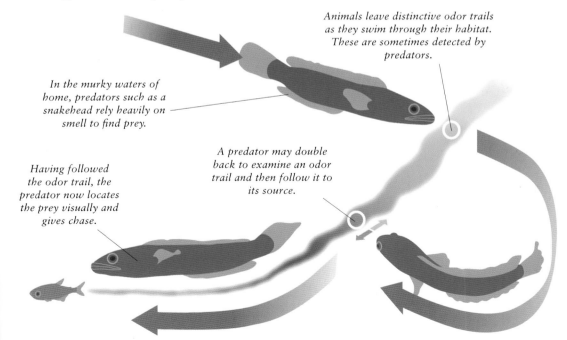

Animals leave distinctive odor trails as they swim through their habitat. These are sometimes detected by predators.

In the murky waters of home, predators such as a snakehead rely heavily on smell to find prey.

A predator may double back to examine an odor trail and then follow it to its source.

Having followed the odor trail, the predator now locates the prey visually and gives chase.

Chemical messages between fish

Fish not only use their sense of smell to find food and stay around their home range, but also to pick up the chemical messages passed from fish to fish. These chemical messages – more correctly called pheromones (from the Greek "pherein" meaning "to carry") – allow fish to gather information about other members of their own species and to find mates. Pheromones also provide a host of other information, allowing fish to eavesdrop on their predators and the other species that share their habitat.

Q: How important is chemical communication for fish breeding?

A: The single most important task in any animal's life is to breed and pass on its genes to its offspring. So when the breeding season comes round, the stakes are high. Fish use pheromones to detect the presence of mates, their readiness to breed and whether they have mated before. Fish are especially sensitive to the presence of sex pheromones, and are able to use them not only to home in on a potential

mate, but also to detect whether their target is ready to breed. This means they are able to concentrate their efforts more effectively. Male goldfish have an unusual trick that they use as part of their courtship display: they swim up to a female and then roll over and urinate over her nostrils. As strange as this seems, it allows the female to assess many things, including the male's genetic make-up, thus preventing her from breeding with a relative.

Q: What happens if these chemical messages are intercepted?

A: Among fish species there are different strategies when it comes to parenthood (see Fish mating systems, page 166 to 189). Some species make considerable investments of time and energy to defend their young, others invest in producing huge numbers of eggs and leave these to fend for themselves. In an ideal world, fish would produce masses of eggs and then defend them, but the energetic

The hunters and the hunted

Surprise is a crucial weapon for many predators, such as catfish. Success depends on the prey being unaware of the danger until it is too late.

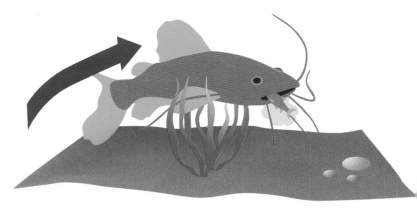

❙ *The predator darts out to capture a smaller fish. The injured prey releases alarm chemicals.*

costs mean that they have to choose between one method or the other. Some species, such as the catfish *Synodontis multipunctatus*, cheat the system by using others to raise their young for them. To do this, they respond to the presence of the sex pheromones of nesting species in their habitat and synchronize their breeding cycles with that species. Then they home in on the source of the sex pheromones and lay their eggs in the nest, leaving their young to be brought up by someone else and neatly side-stepping some of the costs of parenthood.

Q: *Can fish smell fear?*

A: Each species of fish produces its own individual chemical signature, and other fish in the locale can detect these chemical cues and respond accordingly. This not only allows predators to find their prey, but also allows prey to recognize that predators are around and to take evasive action – or so you might assume. Instead, prey fish often respond to the presence of fish predators by approaching them. They can then detect subtle chemical cues that tell them when the predator last ate (and therefore whether it is hungry) and what type of fish the predator has recently been

preying on, all of which tells the prey how much of a threat the predator presents. If and when the predator does attack and injures or captures a fish, this releases an alarm pheromone into the water. Prey species are acutely sensitive to this smell and will rapidly seek cover in response to detecting even tiny concentrations of it. The alarm pheromone is long-lasting, too, and even if the predator has managed to eat the prey, the pheromone continues to act as a chemical marker on the predator, taking away its ability to launch further surprise attacks.

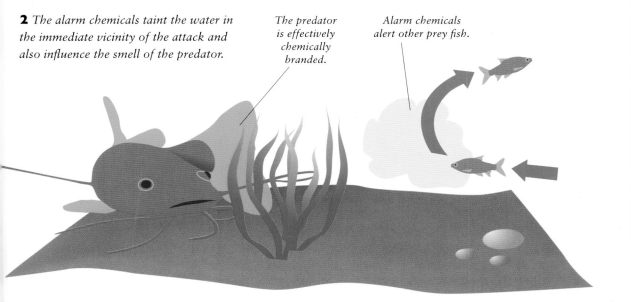

2 *The alarm chemicals taint the water in the immediate vicinity of the attack and also influence the smell of the predator.*

The predator is effectively chemically branded.

Alarm chemicals alert other prey fish.

Chemical cues – taste

For fish that seek their prey under cover of darkness or search among a silty, muddy substrate, vision is of little use in hunting. If they encounter food under these conditions, they need to be able to respond to it quickly, especially if that food has ideas of escaping. As a result, fish that hunt under these conditions make extensive use of their taste cells to provide information. Unlike the sense of smell, taste requires contact between the sensory cell – a taste bud – and the thing being tasted. Many species of fish have an excellent sense of taste. Although lacking a tongue in the sense that we understand it, they have plenty of taste buds and, unusually, these can be found not just in the mouth, but outside it.

Q: Where can fish have taste buds?

A: The idea of tasting food while we eat it is familiar to most of us, but some fish are able to taste their food before they eat it. Catfish, especially, use extra-oral taste buds; the body surface of some species may be covered in as many as 200,000 of these sensory cells. By comparison, the human tongue has around 10,000 taste buds. Many of the catfishes' taste buds are found on their barbels, which extend far beyond their mouths to provide a kind of chemo-sensory radar all around the fish, detecting food hidden out of sight. If the barbels miss the food, then all is not lost – the area around the mouth and indeed much of the body surface of the fish is covered in taste buds. Catfish and many other bottom-dwellers effectively swim along, constantly tasting for food, much like a swimming tongue.

Below: For fish that hunt in the dark, such as this marbled catfish, long barbels are excellent for detecting prey.

Left: The branched barbels of this cuckoo catfish provide it with a huge amount of sensory information.

Right: Barbels are not just for catfish. The zebra danio (Danio rerio) *also comes equipped with these sensors.*

Q: Why do some species have whiskers?

A: These "whiskers," which tend to be sited around the mouth, are more correctly known as barbels. They vary considerably between different fish species but in many cases are covered with a layer of taste receptor cells – taste buds. The whiskers of the zebra danio, for example, are barely visible, whilst the barbels of some catfish are far longer than the body of the fish itself, or are branched to provide comprehensive sensory coverage of tastes in the substrate. Even the modified feeler-like pelvic fins of some gourami species have a covering of sensory cells that may enable the fish to locate food.

Q: Do fish have favorite flavors?

A: Just as with humans, fish have preferences for certain flavors, but these are hard-wired into the animal's genes, so fish within a species tend

Right: The black shark uses barbels to locate food particles hidden in the substrate.

Below: The pearl gourami (Trichogaster leeri) *uses modified pelvic fins to sense its immediate surroundings.*

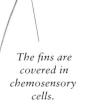

The fins are covered in chemosensory cells.

to have a general preference for certain foods. But there are differences between fish species – herbivorous fish have a taste for the carbohydrates, especially sugars, found in their food, whereas carnivores seek out the amino acids and metabolic compounds found in their common prey.

Q: How else do fish use their taste buds?

A: As well as for foraging, fish also use their sensory systems to detect minute changes in water chemistry. The ability to respond to slight differences in oxygen concentrations is important for a fish's metabolism, for example. Also, in the modern industrial world, these sensory abilities enable fish to avoid the worst pollutants in the aquatic habitat..

Electric communication

All fishes produce a slight electric field as a by-product of the nervous impulses intrinsic to life. However, some species have harnessed and concentrated this ability to enable them to communicate among themselves, to locate prey and, in some cases, to deliver a powerful shock to subdue other animals.

The Amazonian black ghost knifefish (Apteronotus albifrons).

The Asian clown knifefish (Notopterus chitala).

Above: Freshwater fish from different parts of the globe are known for their electric sensory abilities.

Q: Which fishes use electricity and what do they use it for?

A: Normal muscle tissue produces tiny electrical impulses with each movement – this is why hospital monitors can detect the patterns of a human heartbeat. A number of fish species, such as the elephant-nosed fishes of Africa, the ghost knifefish of South America and the knifefish of Asia and Africa, all live in dark or cluttered environments where vision is difficult or impossible. Instead, each has specialized muscle cells arranged along its flanks that produce electrical fields that spread a few inches around themselves, almost like an electrical radar. If an object is detected within this field, the fish is able to distinguish whether it is a rock, a clump of plants or an animal by its electrical conductivity – each conducts electricity differently because of its physical properties. This produces an electrical map of the immediate environment in the fish's brain, helping it to navigate with extreme precision and to find prey in its habitat.

Q: So is electricity used for hunting?

A: Very much so. Some fish, such as *Xenomystus* and *Notopterus*, which lack the ability to produce an electrical field themselves, are able to find hidden prey by detecting the minute electrical signature that all live animals produce, almost as if they were using X-ray vision. They can use this ability to find prey animals hidden deep within the substrate, where they are beyond the detection of most other fishes.

Q: Do they use electricity for anything other than finding their way around?

A: As well as for navigation, elephant-nosed fish use their electrical abilities to communicate with one another. In the simplest example, if two of these fish are hunting in close proximity, one will switch its electrical output to a different frequency so that it does not jam the signal of the other. But the communication becomes much more sophisticated. Males of some species produce specific courtship "songs" during the mating season using electrical impulses to attract females, which can be detected up to 3 feet (1 m) away. Fights and aggression are also mediated through electrical communication. Aggressive individuals increase their rate of electrical discharges before they attack. If the intended victim wishes to signal its submission, it correspondingly decreases its rate of electrical emissions.

Q: Can electric fish zap their prey?

A: A small number of fish, including the electric catfish, have taken the ability to generate electricity even further. They can generate considerable voltages, which they use to stun their prey before eating it and also to discourage any predators that might consider them as a meal.

Below: The electric catfish (Malapterurus electricus) *packs a fearsome electric punch, which it uses to locate objects and stun prey in its naturally dark habitat.*

Detecting prey using electricity

The fields with which electric fish surround themselves are able to detect anything that conducts electricity differently to the surrounding water.

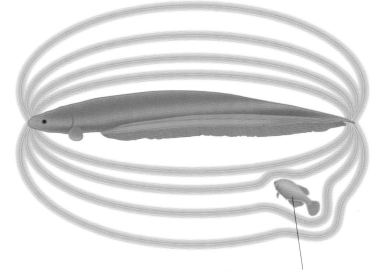

An electric field entirely surrounds this banded knifefish, giving it a 360° mental picture of its world.

A smaller fish disturbs the electric field and is detected. Pinpointed by the electrical radar, it is vulnerable to attack.

Sound detection

Until relatively recently, fish were considered to be silent creatures; they clearly do not have external ears and even though they do have some internal hearing apparatus, it lacks some basic structures. But experiments performed early in the 20th century showed that fish could be trained to emerge to feed on hearing a whistle. Water is an excellent medium for conducting sound; it travels much faster (over four times as fast at about 5,000 feet [1,500 m] per second) and much farther in water than in air, so fish can exploit this to get their message across.

Q: *How do fish hear?*

A: Sound travels as a series of waves or vibrations through the water. Because a fish's body is a similar density to the surrounding water, the waves pass through it. However, in the fish's inner ear there are a number of ear bones known as otoliths. Being bones, these are of a different density to much of the rest of the fish's body. The sound waves cause the otoliths to vibrate and it is this vibration that is picked up by sensory cells in the inner ear and transmitted to the brain. In some species, the swimbladder acts to amplify underwater sounds by picking up the pressure waves of the sound – if you have ever stood near to a loudspeaker and been able to "feel" the sound, especially the low frequency bass, this is essentially the same thing.

Q: *Can fish make noise as well as listen to it?*

A: Fish lack a voice box and so must find other means of making themselves heard. To do this, freshwater fish use two main methods: "stridulation" where they rub their teeth, spines or other skeletal parts together, and "drumming" where muscles around the swimbladder contract rapidly and, as the name suggests, use the swimbladder just like a drum. The fishes' "songs" can range from the quite simple "click" made by loaches (using a similar process to people cracking their knuckles) to the buzzing and

Picking up underwater sounds

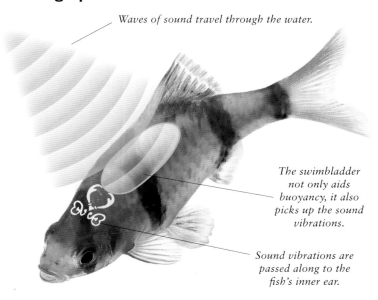

Waves of sound travel through the water.

The swimbladder not only aids buoyancy, it also picks up the sound vibrations.

Sound vibrations are passed along to the fish's inner ear.

growling common among cichlids. Croaking gouramis produce their eponymous sounds using specially adapted pectoral fins.

Q: *What are they telling each other?*

A: Most fish use their sounds for two main purposes: aggression and courtship. Cichlids, such as the jewel *(Hemichromis* spp.*)* and the convict *(Archocentrus nigrofasciatus),* growl if an intruder enters their territory when they are defending young. The click noise produced by some loaches

Above: Skunk loaches (Yasuhikotakia morleti) *click at one another during aggressive encounters.*

Left: Jewel cichlids are extremely noisy in defence of their territories and young.

Below: *Talking catfish* (Platydoras costatus) *produce surprising noises when confronted by a predator.*

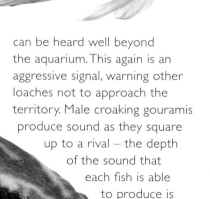

can be heard well beyond the aquarium. This again is an aggressive signal, warning other loaches not to approach the territory. Male croaking gouramis produce sound as they square up to a rival – the depth of the sound that each fish is able to produce is related to its size and ultimately its strength. The stronger the fish, the deeper the aggressive call. But not all fish vocalisations are concerned with aggression; indeed, some evidence suggests that submissive fish produce "appeasement" sounds to try to dissuade an aggressor from launching an attack. Fish may also make sounds during courtship to impress a mate. Talking catfish, which make a surprising noise when taken out of water, may do so to frighten a predator. It is thought that the shock of the sound may just occasionally save the fish's life by causing the predator to drop its prey.

Pressure detection

The lateral line is a unique sensory system that allows fish to detect patterns of water flow over their bodies and waves of pressure from nearby objects. Sensory cells within the lateral line respond to changes in pressure and to changes in water flow to create a kind of sensory field around the fish, in much the same way as described earlier in the electric fishes.

Q: What do fish use the lateral line for?

A: Many fish use their lateral line to find their way about, but this becomes even more important when there is no light, meaning that vision is excluded. For blind cave fish, building up a spatial map of their surroundings represents a particular problem, yet it is one that they solve using

The lateral line

Tiny pores along the flanks of the fish allow water to enter the lateral line canal.

The pores open into the cavity of the lateral line canal.

A jelly-filled sac responds to water movements.

Sensory cells with sensitive "hairs" detect subtle changes in these movements.

Nerve impulses produced by these sensory cells are passed along nerve fibers to the brain.

Water flow and pressure changes can be detected by the lateral line.

their lateral line. When they are introduced to new surroundings, they respond by increasing their

Left: Blind cave fish (Astyanax mexicanus) rely extensively on their lateral line system to orientate within their environment.

swimming speed and tilting their body over onto one side. Although speeding up when you are in a strange environment seems an odd thing to do, the purpose of this is to speed up the flow of water over the fish's body, which makes its lateral line extra sensitive to the new aquascape. Tilting the body over to one side is much like turning your ear towards a faint sound. Tests have shown that the cave

Do not tap the glass

Fish are extremely sensitive to underwater vibrations and can easily be disturbed by sudden high amplitude pressure sounds, such as those caused by a person knocking on the glass wall of an aquarium. Repeated events of this kind can play a major role in stressing the fish.

fish is extremely adept at building up a picture of its environment in its mind using this technique – after all, when did you last see a cave fish bump into something?

Q: Are there fish species that can feel their prey?

A: When a fly accidentally collides with a spider's web, the spider is alerted by the vibrations that travel throughout the web. A similar thing occurs when insects fall onto the surface of water and begin struggling. The butterflyfish (*Pantodon buchholzi*) specializes in this type of prey and sits close to the top of the water, waiting for its next meal. If an insect does blunder into the water, the butterflyfish is able to detect its presence using an exquisitely sensitive lateral line and related sensory pits around the head.

Similarly, nocturnal fish are able to hunt at night using their lateral lines to detect the movements of invertebrates such as shrimps. As a fish swims along, it creates a wake in much the same way as a boat traveling across the surface of the water. And just as with the boat, the wake of a fish diminishes only gradually, leaving a trail for a short time. Predatory fish, such as large catfish, have been shown to be able to follow the wakes of prey fish using their sensitive lateral lines to track and gradually catch up with their unfortunate target.

Below: The butterflyfish (Pantodon buchholzi) *can detect the struggles of drowning insects at the surface.*

Q: Do fish use vibrations to communicate?

A: The bubblenests of fish such as the Siamese fighting fish (*Betta splendens*) are used both to harbor the eggs and, later, as a nursery for the young fish during the first few days of their life. Throughout this time the male defends the offspring, which sit at the surface of the water where they are relatively safe. However, if danger threatens, the male communicates with the young by agitating his fins to produce vibrations on the surface of the water. These are detected by the offspring, who respond by moving towards the comparative safety offered by their protective father.

Chapter 2
Fish learning

Are fish intelligent? Most people think not, believing that goldfish have only a three-second memory. Yet evidence shows that goldfish – indeed all fish species – have a far greater memory than this, plus a remarkable capacity for learning.

Learning – the modification of a response as a result of experience – has been shown in animals ranging from humans to invertebrates. It allows individuals to adapt to different situations and to behave more efficiently, but in order to learn, an animal must have some kind of memory.

Q: *Can fish really learn?*

A: A basic type of learning that has been demonstrated in fishes is the ability to connect two different events. A simple example is the way that aquarium fish associate the appearance of the fishkeeper with the arrival of food. On seeing the former, the fish often begin to swim excitedly at the front of the tank, expecting the imminent addition of food. This is akin in many respects to Pavlov's dogs, where the dogs learned that the ringing of a bell meant that food would shortly arrive and would begin to salivate expectantly. But this is by no means the only connection that fish are able to make. Experiments using male blue gouramis showed that the fish quickly learned that a light being switched on would be followed by the appearance of a female. When the males saw the female they began to display. In time, the males started to display as soon as the light was switched on. Experiments on feeding behavior in archerfish (*Toxotes jaculatrix*) produced a similar response. Archerfish are famous for their ability to spit water at insect targets with incredible accuracy, shooting them down and seizing them as they struggle on the water surface. When researchers switched on a small light before adding an insect to the aquarium, the fish learned to connect the two events, and after a short

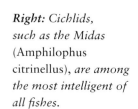

Right: Cichlids, such as the Midas (Amphilophus citrinellus), are among the most intelligent of all fishes.

period of time would start to spit water as soon as the light came on. Although this may seem to bear no relation to the events that a fish might experience in the wild, very often two events are related. It has been observed that fish often growl at one another before they attack (page 30).

Learning that growling usually precedes an attack

means that fish have the chance to back down before they are injured.

Q: *How else can fish learn?*

A: Similar to Pavlovian conditioning is "operant conditioning," where a fish can learn to relate a consequence to a particular behavior pattern. This is the mechanism sometimes used to teach animals to perform tricks – a sea lion may learn that if it jumps through a hoop it is given a reward. Fish have shown an ability to learn a wide variety of tricks in this way, ranging from pushing a lever to obtain food on demand to playing underwater football. Although performing tricks like this may seem frivolous, there is a serious, scientific basis for studying operant conditioning in fishes. By using rewards to encourage a fish to perform an action, we can study, for example, how long it takes the fish to learn under different circumstances, such as different temperatures or oxygen concentrations. By presenting them with a choice of levers to press where only one provides a food reward, we can

▶ Which fish are the most intelligent?

Clearly there is no fish IQ test, but we can make general statements. For example, large, long-lived fish tend to be smarter than small fish with a rapid life cycle, such as guppies. Generally speaking, omnivores and fish that provide parental care also often have real brain power to cope with the tasks that they perform in their lives. Many cichlids and catfish and some gouramis fit the profile and are surprisingly intelligent, being capable of flexible behavior, learning new skills and retaining information for long periods.

look at their ability to discriminate levers based on their color or shape, which tells us a great deal about their evolution. Ultimately, we can also probe the furthest extent of fish intelligence to find out the limits of their ability to learn and to remember. One thing is for sure – the ability to learn new skills should finally lay to rest the mistaken notion that fish have a three-second memory.

Going back to school

In the wild, animals are continuously presented with new challenges and threats. To be successful, they must learn how to cope with these and how to respond to each novel situation. Overwhelming evidence now exists to show that, in common with so-called higher animals, such as mammals, fish are able to learn quickly and effectively in a wide variety of circumstances.

Q: *Do fish inherit knowledge from their parents?*

A: Recognizing what can and what cannot eat you is a vitally important skill for all newborn fish. The problem with learning is that it requires experience, yet an early encounter with a predator is very likely to be the only one. Juvenile fish therefore have an innate ability to recognize predators. This ability is not learned, but instead is encoded in their genes. This genetic information means that young fish of many species are able to recognize the danger posed by large fish according to the configuration of their face and size. The information they use is

simple but important – large eyes and a large mouth spell danger, smaller features are less perilous, even on an equally large fish. The fear shown by the vulnerable fry alters according to these cues. However, avoiding predators is not all about innate recognition; young fish in species that provide parental care, such as cichlids, seem to learn from being herded around by their parents.

Facing danger

Large eyes and mouth spell danger.   *Smaller eyes, but still a risk.*   *Little danger from this friendly face.*

The snakehead's mouth is full of needle-sharp teeth – there is no escape for prey once caught.

Right: The snakehead (Channa sp.) is an out-and-out predator. Its large eyes and mouth equip it perfectly for efficient hunting.

Q: *Can fish learn through experience?*

A: For any fish in the wild, there are hundreds of different foods to eat. Some are simple to catch and eat, while others, such as the faster-swimming water fleas, may be difficult to catch or, in the case of water snails, difficult to eat. When a fish encounters such a prey animal for the first time, it

Above: Tests on the Australian rainbowfish Glossolepis incisus *show that it can memorise tasks for nearly a year without reinforcement.*

Above: Port Hoplo catfish (Megalechis thoracata) *are intelligent and adaptable fish and make excellent parents.*

may take a considerable amount of time to catch and eat it. However, if it continues to come across the same prey animals, the fish will gain experience and learn how to hunt more efficiently. Experiments have shown that fish are remarkably quick learners. For example, if sunfish are given a completely novel and difficult prey animal, they learn the best technique for dealing with it gradually until after five encounters they have reached maximum efficiency. But it is not just learning how to hunt well that is important to wild fish – they also need to learn how to escape when threatened. All fish are born with the instinct to flee from attack, but these abilities may need to be honed if the fish face something new, for instance, a fishing net. Tests on Australian rainbowfish revealed that they rapidly learned the only way to escape when confronted by a net was to find the biggest hole and swim through it.

Q: *How long can fish remember things?*

A: Once a skill has been learned, it needs to be regularly reinforced, otherwise it will be forgotten. The length of time that a new skill can be remembered is known as a "memory window." Memory windows in fish can be extensive; for example, the rainbowfish escapees showed the ability to recall how to escape 11 months after last doing it.

Q: *Are there any fish that use tools?*

A: The ability to use tools is often considered to be strong supporting evidence of animal intelligence. It is seen in apes, monkeys and some birds, but in fish? Surprisingly, there are examples: acaras have been seen to use a leaf to carry their eggs away to safety if they are threatened by predators. Port Hoplo catfish (Megalechis thoracata) are also known to use leaves to carry eggs back into their bubblenest, if these should become detached.

Social learning

Fish seldom live out of contact with others, be they of the same species or entirely different. The actions of other fish in the same environment can provide information for any fish that tunes in to what is happening. For example, if an observer fish sees panic spreading through the other fish in the locality, it may well indicate that a predator is active in the area, so it can use this information to shelter. Similarly, if one fish sees others pecking at the substrate and apparently feeding, it can swim over to join the crowd at the feast.

Q: *Where do fish get their information?*

A: All animals have their own private information, based on their own learning, exploration, and experience. But gaining private information takes energy and time – to learn everything about its environment, a fish would have to investigate all of it, which would usually be a considerable task. As a result, fish often learn from others and use others' experiences to help them to make decisions. This public information is less reliable than finding out things for yourself, but is a much easier option. For example, male swordtails are known to watch fights between other males, a process known as "eavesdropping." They can then judge the strength of each combatant, perhaps avoiding a contest with the winner but taking the opportunity to "kick" the loser while he is down.

Q: *Can fish learn from other fish?*

A: There is plenty of evidence to show that fish can, and do, learn from one another. This process is known as social learning. Guppies, for example, can learn from one another about the location of a hidden food source and in this way, the information spreads throughout entire schools. In fact, social learning in guppies is so powerful that once the fish are taught to swim a lengthy and complicated route to their food patch, this spreads through the school and persists for considerable amounts of time, even though a simpler and shorter route exists. Female mollies (*Poecilia sphenops*) take a great deal of notice of the mate choices of other females, very

Below: Fish in groups, such as these guppies, can find out about their habitat by watching the behavior of others.

Above: Parental catfish (Bagrus meridionalis), *at Chinyamwezi Island, Lake Malawi, not only guard their young, but also bring food back to the nest.*

often choosing to mate with the same male that they have seen the other females mate with. By doing this, the females are trying to ensure that they are mating with a real hotshot. The benefit to them is that their offspring will carry the hotshot's genes, and their sons will hopefully be as sexy as their father – meaning that future females will be sure to choose him. Fish also learn socially about danger: if a fish sees one of its conspecifics fleeing from a particular kind of predator, it quickly learns to avoid that species itself. Juvenile cichlids are also thought to learn from their parents in the same way about what is, and what is not, a danger to them. In relation to this, fish raised by parents seem to recognize predators far better than those raised without parental care. The parental catfish *Bagrus meridionalis* are also thought to teach their offspring what to eat by bringing certain kinds of invertebrate prey to the nest and spitting out the chewed up pieces into the midst of their hungry brood.

▶ Social learning in the aquarium

Social learning is a common phenomenon in the aquarium – as soon as one fish detects that food has been added to the tank, the news travels like wildfire! A similar situation exists when new inhabitants are added to the tank. If the existing fish are accustomed to being fed in the same part of the tank, newcomers can learn where this is, even without actually seeing the food, by picking up cues from their tankmates' behavior.

Orientation

Like all animals, fish move around their habitat. Some, such as barbs or tetras, do so more than predominantly sedentary species, such as catfish, but all need to travel at some time or other to find food or mates. Being able to orientate within the environment is therefore a crucial skill for fishes. It is vital to be familiar with the environment to know where food or danger may be found. And also to know where might be a good refuge, or where your territory is.

Q: *How do they do it?*

A: Although fishes move around a great deal, they tend to demonstrate what is known as site fidelity, so even though they have an entire lake or a huge river to explore if necessary, they usually limit themselves to a particular area of perhaps a few square feet. In order to do this, they use a wide variety of different cues to navigate. For example, they can detect the smell of their own habitat, such as where two rivers converge. On a smaller scale, they can use familiar objects as "landmarks." Fish from

Above: Fish are capable of learning the location of reliable food patches, danger areas and their sleeping grounds.

Right: For the blind cave fish, the lateral line provides a "picture" of its environment.

fairly stable environments, such as lakes and ponds, are most likely to use landmarks, whereas in rivers, where landmarks may be washed away, fish tend to rely on the direction of the current in conjunction with larger landmarks. However, fish navigation is all about having a back-up plan

– what happens if this landmark disappears, or you are chased into unfamiliar territory? As a result, fish are also known to navigate using the earth's magnetic field and, if the sky is clear enough, shallow water fishes, such as mosquitofish, can navigate by the sun. Even in the dark, fish can use their lateral line to "feel" subtle water pressure differences in their habitat. Blind cave fish can detect differences in the shapes of openings in a simple maze, which allows them to choose the right hole to enter for a food reward.

Q: *How good are fish at navigating?*

A: Given the costs associated with getting lost, it's perhaps not surprising that fish are good at navigating. In one experiment, researchers moved some trout 650 feet (200 m) upstream and another group the same distance downstream. In both cases the fish showed an accurate and speedy ability to find their way home. Goldfish are known to be excellent at using landmarks to find their way about and are also able to remember the locations of several different hidden food patches and how to find each of them. Mosquitofish are able to remember areas associated with risk, such as a place where a predator has attacked them before, and consequently avoid such risky/dangerous places. If placed in a radial maze, where a number of corridors protrude from the center, Siamese fighting fish explore them and can learn a good deal of information about the maze, including which arms have food rewards in them and which do not. When placed in the same maze at a later date, the fish go straight to the places where they have learned a food reward is waiting. In terms of distance traveled, it has been shown that cichlids, such as *Pseudotropheus aurora,* can accurately travel over a mile (2 km) to reach home.

Q: *Can fish find their way out of water?*

A: You might imagine that the last place a fish would want to find itself is out of water. And yet, many species are quite adept at crossing land from pool to pool, either to escape predators or leave a shrinking, drying pool. Some species of killifish are good at this, flicking their bodies along the ground in an apparently ungainly way, but showing themselves to be proficient at finding new water bodies. Other species, such as climbing perch and clarias catfish, are far more adept at moving on land to escape unfavorable conditions and can often travel long distances between pools.

Fish out of water

A deeper, more stable pool offers a good home.

A rapidly drying pool means that fish must move on, if they can.

In some killifish, traveling over land is achieved by flicks of the body.

General recognition

While to us it may be difficult to tell apart fish of the same species – even sometimes of different species – it is important for the fishes themselves to be able to do so. For example, fish that reacted in the same way to a predator as to a mate would quickly find itself in trouble. Beyond this, new research shows that fish are capable of some highly impressive recognition abilities.

Q: *What is recognition in fishes?*

A: There are a few main ways in which a fish can recognize others. For example, many species of fish are pre-programmed by their genes to recognize predators and other fish that may be a threat to them or, in the case of species that look after their young, to recognize that the large fish near them (their "parent") is not a threat but that they should keep close by it. Experiments on newly free-swimming convict cichlids have shown that the fry will approach and remain with a model that has conspicuous stripes like their parents. As

well as this, they may form a "recognition template" in very early life – many fish grow up mainly with conspecifics, so they follow a simple rule of "I am the same as the fish around me," much like the ugly duckling tale. Unfortunately, this is not foolproof – swordtails that are raised with guppies prefer to associate with guppies in later

life. Recognition abilities may also be learned; for example, if a fish sees a predator attacking another fish, it can learn that the predator represents danger and can take action to avoid it.

Below: Convict cichlid fry are strongly drawn towards bold stripes, be they on a parent or even a black-and-white model.

hear them talking and recognize a regional accent, so you have an idea where they are from. Only when you get pretty close can you work out if you have met them before. A similar process occurs with fish – they recognize species, size, sex and population and, in some cases, they can recognize detail minute enough to know exactly who they are dealing with.

Q: *What other things can fish recognize?*

A: It is in fishes' interests to recognize some other characteristics as well. Members of the carp family, such as barbs, can recognize which fish are poor competitors and show a preference for associating with them, presumably knowing that when it comes to feeding time, they themselves will have the upper hand. They can also recognize which individuals are behaving oddly – these are important to avoid if you are a schooling fish as they can attract predators. Cyprinids also recognize fish that are obviously ill or parasitized and use this information to decide whether to associate with them or not, because it is in their own interests to stay away if the condition is catching.

Q: *What and who do they recognize?*

A: Fish are capable of both a general kind of recognition, say, the ability to recognize members of their own species or predators, and a much more specific recognition of individual fish (see page 44). In fact, fish are capable of quite a few different levels of recognition. To illustrate this, imagine walking down the street

Above: Fish can distinguish between other species, deciding whether they are dangerous or a possible competitor.

and seeing a figure at a distance. You would probably work out first that they were from the same species as yourself – a human – and as you got nearer you might recognize various other characteristics, maybe their height, age, and sex. Next, you might

Specific recognition

Some of the most remarkable discoveries about fish in recent years have centered on their clear ability to recognize particular individual fish. Incredible as this may seem, this capacity to distinguish specific individual identities has now been demonstrated in a huge variety of fish.

Q: *Can fish recognize their relatives?*

A: The ability to recognize kin is extremely important in many species. In one basic example, guppies have been shown to avoid eating their own offspring

while happily munching everyone else's. Parental firemouth cichlids can also recognize their own fry; remarkably, they will kidnap the fry of others and put these on the edge of their own school of offspring so that they, and not their own young, are in harm's

way – a kind of "cichlid shield." Almost all fish are thought to be able to recognize their own siblings, which is important because it prevents the possibility of inbreeding. Female rainbowfish are particularly good at this, avoiding their own brothers

Left: Parental cichlids, such as these firemouths (Thorichthys meeki) in the Rio Dulce, Mexico, can distinguish between their own and unrelated fry.

A cichlid shield

By adding unrelated fry to their own brood, parental fish can give their own offspring the best chance of survival. The 'kidnapped' fry dilute the risk of attack to their step-siblings.

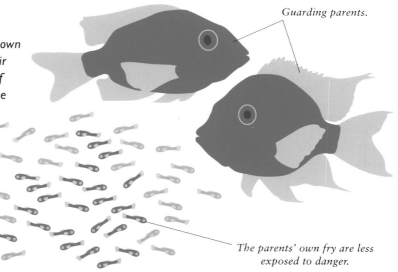

Guarding parents.

"Kidnapped" fry from an unrelated brood are placed in the riskiest positions.

The parents' own fry are less exposed to danger.

for this reason, but forming kin schools with their sisters and half-sisters, which allows the possibility for mutual benefits through co-operation.

Q: What about recognizing unrelated fish?

A: A large number of fish species choose their "friends," learning to recognize particular individuals and sticking with them over considerable periods of time in a phenomenon known as "familiarity." This can have many benefits for all concerned: familiar fish are less likely to fight over food and are better able to survive predator attacks because they form more cohesive schools. Some fish choose their "friends" extremely carefully; guppies prefer to associate with individuals that co-operate with them in risky circumstances, while sunfish choose to be with individuals with whom they have successfully hunted in the past. Male guppies, ever footloose and fancy free, avoid females that they have met before and with whom they are familiar, preferring to mate with the new girls in town. In doing so, they are able to spread their genes further than would otherwise be possible.

Q: Can fish have "friends" in other species?

A: The ability of fish to recognize particular individuals is not limited to fish of the same species. Fish that have been tankmates for any length of time repeatedly interact with one another and become familiar. This can occur even when the fish would not be naturally found together in the same habitat. Stories abound of fish that become attached to one another and that even pine if separated. One such anecdote refers to an African grey knifefish (*Xenomystus nigri*) and climbing perch (*Ctenopoma kingsleyae*), which not only tolerated one another but seemed to co-operate at feeding time to keep the other tank inhabitants at bay. Another

Above: Female rainbowfish prefer to gather with their sisters and half-sisters, but actively avoid their own brothers.

episode concerns an oscar cichlid (*Astronotus ocellatus*) and a triangle cichlid (*Uaru amphiacanthoides*) that were raised together and cohabited peacefully for months. When the oscar was removed to a new tank in an attempt to pair it with another, the triangle cichlid pined and refused to eat for several days until the owner, guessing the problem, finally relented and returned the oscar to the tank. The triangle cichlid immediately recovered its former perkiness and its appetite, and the two remained inseparable ever after.

Chapter 3
Rhythms of life

All life on earth is governed by rhythms, such as the day-night cycle or the changing of the seasons, and fish are no exception. These rhythms predict when fish are most active, when they eat and sleep and when they migrate and breed.

Fish have three main aims over the course of their lives: to eat, to avoid being eaten, and to reproduce themselves. The way they approach these functions varies from species to species, but it is all governed by rhythms. Three main rhythms affect underwater life: the day-night cycle caused by the earth spinning on its axis and the annual cycle of the earth orbiting the sun are particularly important to freshwater fish, while the cycle of the tides affects only marine fish and estuarine species.

Q: *How do fish keep track of time?*

A: In each case, the behavior of the fish is governed by an internal biological clock that is synchronized to cyclic changes in the environment by so-called "zeitgebers," or "time givers." These are signals that act on the animal's biological clock, such as the arrival of dawn or the rise in temperatures that herald spring, and they re-set it and keep it accurate.

The biological clock starts to develop early in a fish's life; in fact it is usually almost fully developed by the time the fish hatches from the egg.

Q: *How accurate are these internal clocks?*

A: If an animal is taken from the wild and kept in a constant environment for a time, say, in constant light or at

Right: As with most fish, the activity patterns of red-tailed catfish (Phractocephalus hemioliopterus) are governed by daily as well as annual rhythms.

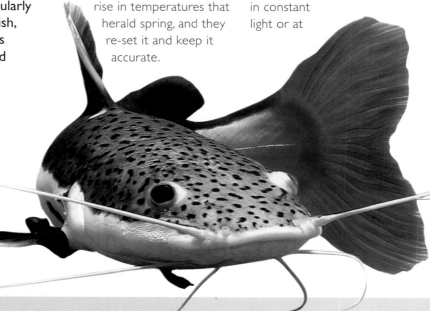

Above: *The life cycle of wild neon tetras (Paracheirodon innesi) is closely tied in with annual patterns of flood and drought in their native rivers.*

a constant temperature, its rhythmic behavior will gradually decrease in the absence of those vital zeitgebers to update its biological clock.

However, the internal clock is quite robust; depending on the species, it can take anything up to six weeks for a fish to lose its connection to the rhythms of the natural world completely. To see fish behaving naturally in the home aquarium, it is therefore necessary to replicate the natural day-night fluctuations and annual temperature cycles that the fish would experience in the wild.

Q: What other rhythms do fish respond to?

A: Fish must also respond to other cycles, including the need to forage when hungry and the need to synchronize their activities with those of their prey and the activities of rivals or mates from within their own species. While the environment imposes its own rhythms on fish, the animals also undergo a life cycle from birth to death as they hatch, grow, reproduce, and die. In species with a distinct spawning season, the population is seen to be structured into year groups of different ages and sizes. In those species that spawn all year round, the cycles are less clear and the community will consist of fish from a range of different ages and sizes.

A life in the day

Most tropical fish species are diurnal, meaning they are active during the day, when the light allows them to use their eyesight to hunt and avoid predators. In the tropics, day and night are of similar length, so the fish have a great deal of activity to pack into 12 hours. As a result, the aquatic environment in the rivers and lakes there are a whirl of color and activity. Large schools of fish gather on the edges of weed beds and, at the surface, larger fish prowl the deeper open water areas.

Q: Do fish have a daily schedule?

A: For fish in the wild, the first few hours of the day are taken up by voracious foraging in order to top up their energy levels after a night with little feeding. Just after dawn, lake fish move into the shallow-water littoral zones, which are rich in invertebrate prey. Having satiated themselves, they may move back to the relative safety of deeper, open water during the afternoon. Alternatively, younger fish, especially, may seek out hot spots at the water surface or in very shallow water, where

they can bask in the sunshine. Spending time in warmer water accelerates their metabolism and speeds up the process of converting food into growth. Larger fish have fewer natural enemies. Nonetheless, fish are at great risk from predators such as birds while basking. As birds are primarily visual hunters, they pose the greatest risk during daylight hours. The first realization that a fish-eating bird is at large may be a shadow passing overhead. As a result, fish tend to be extremely sensitive to movement above the

water surface, even those species that have been kept in captivity for years – old habits die hard. Basking fish are even more acutely aware of the danger and dart into deeper water at the first sign of movement nearby.

Q: Do fish use the sun to navigate?

A: Fish often have stereotypical patterns of movement each day, which they follow throughout their lives. This might involve moving between their overnight

A day in the lake

Fish often follow fairly predictable daily migration paths, visiting favored feeding grounds before returning to overnight resting sites.

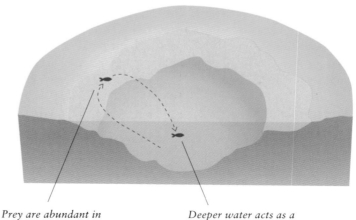

Prey are abundant in warm, shallow waters.

Deeper water acts as a refuge from many predators.

Going by the sun

1 *The early morning sun, rising in the east, gives the fish a reference point to help them to find their way out to their feeding grounds.*

2 *By late afternoon, the sun has crossed to the west. Fish use this to update their internal clocks and to help them navigate back to resting places.*

refuge to one or more foraging grounds and back again during the course of the day. To do this they can navigate by the sun, using its position in the sky to assist them in deciding their traveling direction.

Q: What do nocturnal fishes do during the day?

A: While the diurnal fishes bustle around the habitat in perpetual motion, their nocturnal counterparts spend the day in concealment, waiting for dusk. Fish such as the upside-down catfish (*Synodontis nigriventris*) hold station underneath sunken

wood or rock in their familiar inverted position throughout the day, occasionally darting out for food but concentrating most of their feeding effort in the hours of darkness. In the deeper waters of the African Rift Valley, where very little light penetrates,

Synodontis and other adult catfish are active throughout the full 24 hours. However, the juveniles, which live in shallower water, show the typical nocturnal pattern and hide during daylight.

Left: Nocturnal fish, such as this upside-down catfish (Synodontis nigriventris), *rest up and await the arrival of dusk.*

49

Night life

At night, the underwater world is a very different place. Much like a human city, the hustle and bustle of the day is replaced by a quiet, slightly eerie scene. Also, just as in a city, the night can be a dangerous time: although visual predators, such as birds, are not active, a variety of nocturnal predators are out hunting, hoping to take advantage of unwary fish. The amount of light that penetrates the water depends on the phase of the moon, but even so, beyond the uppermost layers, pitch darkness descends. At the same time, temperatures begin to drop after the heat of the day, and plants, which are no longer photosynthesizing, use up oxygen in the water.

Q: Do fish sleep?

A: As day gives way to night, fish seek out places to rest. Fish have no eyelids and so cannot close their eyes. Nonetheless, they do exhibit two other hallmarks of sleep – they stop moving and their breathing slows. Although many of the fishes' major predators take the opportunity to rest during the evening, new threats emerge. In the streams of Trinidad, home to the guppy, large prawns leave their daytime hiding places to scour the bottom for scraps of food and even unwary sleeping fish. They do not need light to hunt, using their powerful sense of smell instead. As a result, the fish cannot afford to relax completely and they do not; their lateral lines are able to detect movement in the water nearby. If

a predator approaches, they dart away with a sudden flick of their tails. Many diurnal fishes change color during the night, adopting less showy colors. The pencilfish (*Nannostomus beckfordi*) changes its pattern from a horizontal band along the length of its body during the day, to two or three vertical bands. This helps it blend in with the aquatic plants in which it shelters overnight.

Patterns of pencilfish

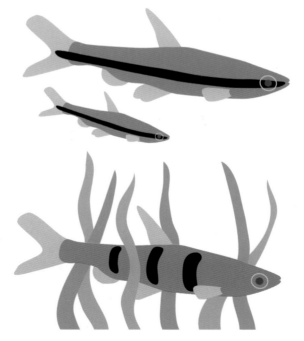

Day: The single longitudinal stripe of the pencilfish helps members of the same species to recognize each other throughout the day.

Night: At night, the fish adopt a different color pattern, which may help with camouflage in the weed beds where they rest.

Q: Do parental fish get a chance to sleep?

A: Not all diurnal fishes get the chance to sleep once night falls. Parental fish guarding vulnerable eggs and young maintain their vigils throughout the night. Using infra-red lighting, which is undetectable to the fish, researchers have been able to watch how convict cichlids keep fanning the brood to maintain the flow of precious oxygen to the developing offspring. As oxygen levels drop during the night, diligent parents cannot afford to take time off at this critical stage. As well as keeping up with the housekeeping, the threat of predators means that the parents

Below: Predators, such as this duckbill catfish (Sorubim lima) *patrol at night, hunting for prey by sensing smells and vibrations.*

Right: Brooding cichlid parents forgo sleep to provide continuous care for their young during their early life.

must keep up their defensive efforts all night.

Q: How do nocturnal fish find their way around?

A: The pressures of life during the day have led some fish species to switch to being nocturnal – being active at night. In this way, they can avoid both visual predators such as birds and the mass of competitors. The one disadvantage, of course, is that there is little light at night. Many

of the species that opt for the nocturnal way of life normally live in light-deprived areas anyway, such as catfish. These fish are often characterized by having small eyes and using senses other than vision to guide them on their hunting forays, especially smell and taste. Seeking the chemical cues produced by their prey means that many nocturnal predators swim slowly and more deliberately than diurnal fishes that hunt by sight.

The twilight zone

For fish, dawn and dusk are times of great activity, comparable to the rush hour familiar to human commuters the world over. As the sun rises, diurnal fish move from deeper water where they often rest, to begin foraging in the first light. Nocturnal fish make the opposite journey, returning to deeper water and to concealment to wait out the coming day. Dawn also triggers spawning in a huge variety of fish, possibly because it offers a window of opportunity for parents, lowering the risk of the eggs being eaten by either nocturnal fish or their diurnal counterparts. Later, as the sun starts to set, the process seen at dawn is reversed: diurnal fishes migrate to deeper water or into vegetation and the nocturnal fishes emerge.

Q: How do levels of light in the habitat relate to fishes' activity?

A: Light levels are directly related to fishes' activity patterns. The decrease in light levels that happens each evening as the sun sets prompts changes in fishes'

behavior. For example, schools start to break up as visual contact becomes more difficult, and fish start to swim more slowly. Remarkable changes occur in the fishes' eyes at this time. Cells are repositioned in the retina, enabling the fish to see in very low light levels. But the changes in fish behavior that accompany dawn and dusk are not controlled solely by light levels. The fishes' internal clocks dictate that they begin the transition to a new phase of activity well in advance of sunrise or sunset. If they are kept on a consistent night and day regime, fish in an aquarium will switch from night to day behavior and vice versa at the correct time even if no light reaches them for a few days. After this, the absence of the zeitgeber (see page 46) will cause the timings to go awry.

Q: I've heard that dawn and dusk are critical times for fish. Why is this?

A: One reason why dawn and dusk are so hectic is because this is when visual predators, such as pike cichlids, are at their most active. A recent study showed

Diurnal fish activity cycles

Diurnal fishes rest at night, but their activity levels start to increase before dawn.

Activity levels peak mid-morning as the fish feed, then gradually decrease throughout the day.

By dusk, activity levels are already low, and the resting fish remain very still during the night.

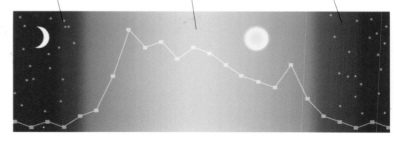

that predatory fish catch 60-70% of their food at these times. The critical thing for a predator is to get as close as possible to its prey without being seen before launching an attack, so predators use the half light to close the gap between themselves and their prey. As a consequence, a visual "arms race" exists between predators and their prey: the most successful predators are those with the best eyesight, because they catch the most food. These individuals are more likely to have offspring and to pass on their excellent eyesight to them. Set against this, only those prey that are able to see well enough to avoid the predators in the gloom survive to reproduce. As a result, both predator populations and

Above: Predators such as the arowana (Osteoglossum bicirrhosum) *are perfectly geared for hunting in the twilight.*

Below: Twilight is a risky time for young cichlids, and their parents must be especially alert (here Neolamprologus tretocephalus).

their prey gradually evolve better and better eyesight in response to one another.

Q: *How do parental fishes respond to the approaching night?*

A: As the afternoon moves into evening, parental cichlids prepare by corralling their offspring into tightly packed groups. They dig pits in the substrate and transfer the young into them for the night. In fact, the task of constructing the pits is undertaken well before dusk, as the fishes' internal clocks inform their activity and allow them to do the housekeeping in good time. The parents have little option but to maintain their vigilance throughout the night; keeping the young safe is a 24-hour job.

Feeding time

Fish in the wild synchronize their activity with the availability of food each day, often visiting a particular location at a specific time. These foraging cycles exist when the availability of food is predictable in time and space and the fish can rapidly satisfy their feeding requirements. As well as reaping rich food rewards by learning when and where food may be available, fish also benefit by reducing their risk of predation – fish are extremely vulnerable while feeding because their levels of vigilance drop.

Q: Do fish know when it's dinner time?

A: As we have seen (page 46), fish have an internal clock. The first real evidence of this came during the 20th century when experimenters showed that if goldfish were fed every day at the same time, they would start to behave in an anticipatory way – for example, increasing their activity and spending more time at the feeding site – shortly before their mealtime. More recently, researchers in Canada have shown that fish can

become accustomed to feeding at different times of the day in different parts of their aquarium, learning to associate feeding at certain times at specific places.

Q: When do fish forage in the wild?

A: The simple answer is whenever there is food. Wild fish tend to show typical daily foraging patterns, especially adults who, unlike juveniles, can sometimes satisfy their daily feeding requirements in one intense feeding session. As we have seen (page 48), many smaller lake fishes tend to move from deep waters early in the morning to feed in the rich littoral zones

Above: Grazers, such as this Petrotilapia sp., have to feed steadily throughout the day to maintain their condition.

along the lake shore before returning to the deeper water in the afternoon. Similarly, river fish may move into the main channel to feed on drifting prey, returning to slacker water once they have completed feeding. In each case, the pattern of foraging is dictated by the food, so predators often step up their activity at twilight to take advantage of low light levels. Blind cave fish show typical daily rhythms, even though there is no difference between night and day in their permanently dark world. In fact, the reason they show

these rhythms is that the cave fish feed on the guano and dislodged cave insects that are provided by the bats that share their subterranean world and which leave en masse at dusk each day. The bats peak activity cycles are reflected in those of the cave fish.

Q: *Do fish match their behavior to changing food levels?*

A: Many Rift Lake cichlids feed by browsing on the algal film that covers the rocks close to shore. As with all plants, algae photosynthesize, converting the sunlight they receive into plant sugars, which they store and use as energy. The plants produce most sugars, and are therefore very valuable as a food source, in the early afternoon when the sun is at its most powerful. A study on the cichlid *Tropheus moorii* in Lake Tanganyika showed that the fish concentrate their foraging activity primarily between 12 noon and 4 pm, even to the extent of aggressively defending small feeding territories. At all other times, levels of aggression and territoriality are much lower – there being less at stake – and the fish gather into large groups.

> ## ▶ Feeding fish in the aquarium
>
> In the wild, fish can browse throughout the day on a variety of different foods. Aquarium fish, however, are dependent upon having their food provided. Modern flake or pellet foods for domestic fish are rich in nutrients and provide an excellent diet for fish. Supplementing the diet with fresh and frozen foods can help to keep fish in peak condition by replicating the dietary variation experienced by their wild counterparts.

Foraging in a river

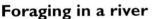

Fish may benefit most by dividing their time between different parts of the river.

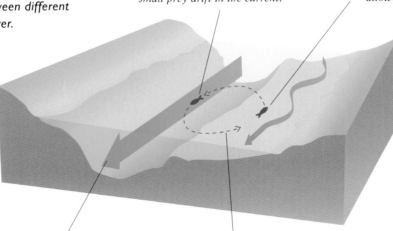

Rich pickings are available in the main channel as myriads of small prey drift in the current.

Out of the main flow, water in the shallows can warm up considerably, allowing fish to bask.

Although rich in food this is also where most danger lurks.

Fish move between the feeding grounds and the shallows to speed up their digestion or to escape predators.

Swimming in the rain

The tropics, home to so many fish species, have distinct and predictable seasons. During the rainy season, the aquatic habitat is transformed by huge volumes of water. For around four months, the Amazon region experiences torrential rain. This, combined with the accompanying meltwater from the Andes, causes the river to rise by anything up to 40 feet (12 m) and to flood beyond its banks as much as 10 miles (16 km) from the main channel. It covers thousands of square miles of floodplains, which may remain submerged for several months. For fish, the annual flood brings rich pickings in terms of food and they rapidly build up fat reserves and grow. For this reason, the species that live in rivers in the tropics very often time their breeding to coincide with the beginning of the rainy season, thus ensuring that their offspring hatch and prosper among the flooded forests.

A year in an Asian river

Rainy seasons and dry seasons produce enormous changes in the river, which in turn affect fish behavior.

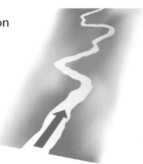  

1 *The migration of adult clown loaches takes place just before the peak in the rainy season.*

2 *After spawning, the newly hatched loaches can exploit the glut of food on the flooded lands.*

3 *Gradually the huge numbers of young disperse. Some are harvested for the aquarium trade.*

Q: How do fish respond to the annual rainy season?

A: The end of the dry season is marked in many regions of South America, Asia, and Africa by an upstream migration of adult fish. For example, large adult clown loaches (*Chromobotia macracanthus*) move up the channels of the rivers where they live in Sumatra to spawn. The young hatch at the beginning of the rains and grow rapidly on the flood plains. In the early weeks of their life, they lack the power to swim against the current and drift gradually downstream, eventually reaching the areas of the river from where their parents set out a few months before. The initial adult migration therefore counteracts the potential problem of larvae drifting out of the river entirely, and it is also suggested that moving upstream to spawn reduces the risk of predation to the eggs and young. Some migrations are thought to be quite substantial, with larger species moving miles upstream. Even the smaller fish travel considerable distances.

Q: How do fish match their life cycles to the changing seasons?

A: The floodplains can remain underwater for months, but as the wet season gives way to the dry, water levels start to drop. Gradually the river returns to its original course, leaving thousands of isolated sink holes and ponds in its wake. These can be extremely tough environments, low in oxygen and fraught with danger as the river's predators become constrained to small pools. In the ditches of Southeast Asia, the male croaking gourami builds a bubblenest when the water levels are at their lowest and temperatures well above 79°F (26°C). If he has timed it right, the rains will arrive with their bounty by the time the young have developed sufficiently to feed on larger food items. Even back in the main river channels, conditions can be tough and food

Right: The arrival of the rains and the dramatic changes they bring about in the river present fish with both problems and opportunities.

scarce during the dry season. However, most of the returning fish have built up considerable reserves during the floods to see them through this period. Those surviving fry that hatched at the beginning of the wet season are now adult, awaiting their turn to spawn with the coming of the next rains.

Q: How can I persuade fish from these habitats to come into breeding condition?

A: As so many of the fish kept in aquariums, including several of the scatter-spawning tetras and barbs, spawn during

the rainy season, it is often well worthwhile attempting to simulate their natural conditions, especially when trying to persuade difficult species to breed. By the end of the dry season, water levels are low and the amount of dissolved organic matter in the water means that oxygen levels are also low. The advent of the rains brings a change in water chemistry as the soft rainwater dilutes the stale river water. Water levels and oxygen levels rise and the colder rainwater causes the temperature to drop. Finally, food ranging from infusorians to the fry of other species is suddenly in abundance.

Changing seasons

The dramatic changes that
are part of the annual cycle in
many tropical rivers provide
challenges and opportunities
for the fish that live in them.
The floods bring an annual
explosion of nutrients and
fish exploit this opportunity
by timing their breeding
to coincide with them.
In fact, this strategy of
breeding when the
conditions are at
their most suitable
for the fry is the crux
of all fishes' annual cycles.

Above: *The colors of
this firemouth cichlid
(Thorichthys meeki) are
especially brilliant during
the breeding season.*

Q: How do fish of temperate zones time their breeding seasons?

A: Some of the subtropical
species kept by aquarists, including
White Cloud Mountain minnows
(*Tanichthys albonubes*), use
different cues to determine the
best time to breed. North and
south of the tropics, day length
changes throughout the year;
the days are longer in summer
than in winter. In addition, water
temperatures are higher at
certain times of year. The fish use
these as cues to decide when to
breed. The typical pattern among
subtropical and temperate fish,
such as sunfish, is to breed during
spring. This allows the fry to take
advantage of the increase in
food associated with spring and
summer, in conjunction with the
higher temperatures that allow
them to grow large enough to
survive the harsh winter.

Q: Do all fish have breeding seasons?

A: Breeding seasons are not
for everyone. A better strategy
for fish that live in stable
environments can sometimes be
to breed throughout the year,
spreading the risk by producing
multiple broods of young. This
pattern is seen in many wild
Central American cichlids, for
instance. However, the energetic
costs of breeding are extreme,
even more so if, like many cichlids,
parental care is provided. So,
although breeding may occur all
year round to a greater or lesser
extent, there are peak breeding
periods. For wild Nicaraguan

convict cichlids, this occurs during the dry season, roughly from January to May. Some fish species, including the guppy, have lifespans that may be measured in weeks rather than years and this negates the point of a breeding season. Female guppies therefore produce young every four weeks or so. The number and size of the offspring in each batch is determined by the conditions – plenty of food especially allows larger broods.

Q: What cues trigger spawning in lake fishes?

A: Although lakes undergo less obvious seasonal changes than rivers, major transformations are occurring beneath the water surface, even in the huge Rift Lake systems. During the cooler months from June to August, a southeasterly wind known as the "mwera" blows. It creates currents in the waters of Lake Malawi and causes nutrient-rich waters to arise from the depths. This upwelling of nutrients boosts the food chain from algae to zooplankton and upwards and provides excellent conditions for larval fish to feed. As a result there is a peak in fish spawning at this time. A second peak in the fishes' breeding season

Above: Wild fish such as these convict cichlids must pack their year's breeding efforts into a few short months.

occurs at the end of the rains in April and May, possibly for similar reasons, as parental fish aim to time their breeding efforts to coincide

with peak growth conditions for the young.

White Cloud Mountain minnow (Tanichthys albonubes).

When water conditions are favorable, fish switch their attention to spawning. The female (here) develops a rounded belly full of eggs.

Fish out of water – drought

Killifish, or pupfish, are quite possibly the most remarkable group of vertebrates living today, comprising around 100 species of small fish grouped into the family Cyprinodontidae. They have a wide distribution range, encompassing the Americas, Africa, Europe, and Asia. Among these is the only vertebrate species known to be capable of self fertilization, the mangrove killifish (*Kryptolebias marmoratus*). Male killifish can be dazzlingly colorful, but the family is most famous for the ability of some of its species – the annual killifish – to survive as eggs through prolonged droughts – truly fish out of water.

Right: The life cycle of some species of killifish includes a period where the highly specialized eggs (inset, showing "hooks") survive out of water.

Q: What habitats do annual killifish live in?

A: In arid regions, brief rainy seasons give rise to temporary pools of various sizes, ranging from broad, shallow oases to tiny puddles created by an elephant's footprint. These exist for perhaps a few weeks, dwindling under the hot sun until they disappear. Incredibly, the killifish have succeeded in adapting to this habitat, where they briefly flourish, growing to maturity, spawning and dying within weeks.

Q: How do the killifish eggs survive drying out?

A: The killifishes' secret is in their superbly adapted eggs. The shell is layered to protect the developing embryo, specifically to prevent it from drying out. When the rain arrives it acts as a trigger, causing the embryo inside to begin to grow. Until this happens the embryo remains in a state of suspended animation, properly known as diapause, for months or even years. The fish also have a mechanism to prevent a brief shower from activating the eggs at the wrong time and causing the local population to die out; a proportion of the eggs in each batch will not hatch until soaked and dried a second time. It is

Left: Killifish can survive in some of the toughest conditions, such as here in a shallow roadside ditch in Mozambique.

not just the presence of water that promotes hatching either. A drop in the level of dissolved oxygen and an increase in carbon dioxide in the water are thought to instigate the final stage of hatching. These patterns of dissolved gases in the water are some indication of the presence of infusorians, which provide the larva's first meal.

Q: *What is the life cycle of these killifish?*

A: When the rains arrive, those embryos that succumb to temptation and hatch are immediately engaged in one of the most accelerated life cycles of all vertebrate animals. The race is now on to complete their life cycle before the pool dries up. Unlike most fish, killifish larvae are not provisioned with yolk sacs and therefore need to hunt for food as soon as they hatch. From this moment forward they feed voraciously and, if conditions allow, grow extremely rapidly; fish of the genus *Nothobranchius* are reputed to reach maturity after as little as 30 days. Males, in particular, are aggressive as they have much at stake – one breeding season to get it right and plenty of competition to contend with. This urgency is also reflected in the brilliant colors typical of the male annual killifish, each contender hoping to attract as many females as possible to mate. If and when he is successful, the pair swim side by side, delivering fertilized eggs into the muddy bottom of their home. Although annual killifish can live for over a year in the aquarium, their wild counterparts seldom survive long after spawning – having laid their eggs, their mission is complete and their life is curtailed by the seasonal drying of the pool once more.

The life cycle of annual killifish

I *As water levels drop, a breeding pair deposits eggs.*
2 *Deep in the mud, the eggs survive the drought conditions.*
3 *The first rains trigger a partial hatching.*
4 *Drought returns.*
5 *Returning rains produce another hatching.*
6 *The fry grow rapidly in their race against time.*

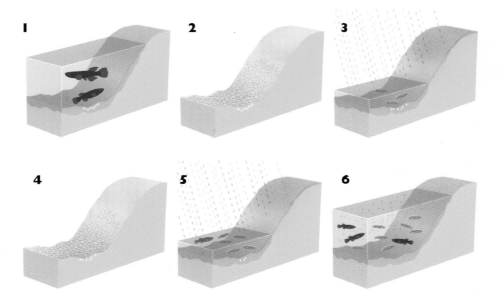

The fish and the egg

All fish begin life inside an egg. Even livebearers start out as an egg, hatching inside their mother before being born; most are ovoviviparous, rather than truly viviparous. Each egg is a complex chemical soup of proteins, fats, and sugars, with a genetic code to fit it all together, and it is all contained within a protective but gas-permeable shell. Life begins for a fish the moment the egg is fertilized, an event that occurs for many species in the water column as the egg drifts slowly towards the bottom. From this point onwards the pace of development is relentless – eggs are an excellent and nutritious food source and it is a race for each developing embryo to hatch before being found by a hungry predator.

Q: What are the first few hours of life like?

A: When the sperm and egg first fuse and a new life begins, the embryo consists of just one single cell. For many familiar tropical fish, it takes around three days for the egg to hatch. These 72 hours are arguably the most active period of a fish's life. The single cell splits into two soon after fertilization and about 20 minutes later, it divides into four. This rate of division and growth continues for the next few hours until the embryo can be seen within the egg by the naked eye. It appears as a bump on one side of the large round "globe" inside the egg. The globe is the yolk sac, the provision left by the mother fish for her offspring. It is the yolk sac that fuels the early development of the embryo. As the embryo continues to expand, it starts to grow around the outside of the yolk sac, eventually enveloping it within a thin layer of cells. The main body of the embryo is visible as a raised band curling around part of the yolk sac. It may not look like much, but in the first six hours of life, the embryo has gone from a single cell to tens of thousands, all with the original DNA blueprint.

Development in the egg

The early stages of a fish's life are a period of dramatic change from a blob of cells to a miniature copy of its parents.

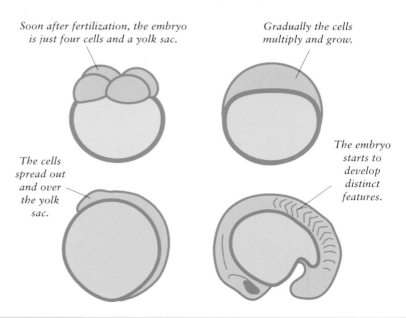

Soon after fertilization, the embryo is just four cells and a yolk sac.

Gradually the cells multiply and grow.

The cells spread out and over the yolk sac.

The embryo starts to develop distinct features.

the fish curls inwards to form a tube that will eventually become the fish's backbone. The major organs – the heart, the liver, and the brain – develop apace. After a further 24 hours, the embryo appears impatient to enter the big wide world; tiny muscles are twitching, the heart is beating and eyes can be clearly seen. The embryo is almost ready to hatch. Curled tightly round the yolk sac, the egg offers little room for further growth. The next stage of life occurs beyond the egg, in open water.

Q: Are all these cells the same?

A: Until now, all the cells were identical copies of one another, but a functioning animal has many different kinds of cells – skin cells, blood cells, nerve cells, etc. At this point in development, different genes switch on within different cells of the embryo and change the course of development for that cell and its subsequent lineage. This process, known as differentiation, is irreversible; once the genes have instructed a cell to become, for example, a brain cell, then its fate is mapped

Above: A male Sturisoma *catfish tends to his eggs. The embryos can be clearly seen inside them.*

out. Gradually the fates of all the embryo's cells are determined and the mosaic of diverse cell types continue to develop, creating specific tissues and organs in the embryo's body.

Q: How does a group of cells develop into a fish?

A: From being a blob of cells, after one day the embryo begins to look like what it is – a fish. A ribbon of cells along the length of

***Above:** The eggs of the desert goby* (Chlamydogobius eremius) *attached to a stone.*

63

Larva life

When the embryo emerges from the egg it becomes known as a larva. The first stage of its life is over but the pace of its development is maintained. The odds of a fish surviving past the larval stage are often tiny but if it is to have any chance, it must grow – and quickly.

Q: What happens during the first few hours following hatching?

A: The newly hatched larva is still some way from living an independent life and hunting for its own food. After hatching, most fishes continue to absorb food for the first few days from the yolk sac. During this time, the larva's body continues to develop. The system of muscles in the body links up with the nervous system and the brain. For the first time, the fish is able to co-ordinate its movements, although while it continues to feed on the yolk sac, the larva cannot swim freely. Some larval fishes, keen not to draw unwelcome attention to themselves, remain very still at this stage. Others, particularly those with parents to protect them, continually twitch and wriggle,

The newly hatched fish

The yolk sac is a rich source of food, but lasts only for a few days.

Instead of a series of different fins, most newly hatched fry have a continuous fin, like that of a tadpole.

The sensory systems are developing, but the fish is not yet capable of hunting or dodging predators.

working their developing muscles like a fledging bird.

Q: When does the larval fish start to feed itself?

A: Once the yolk supply is exhausted the larval fish must find food rapidly. Fish at this stage obviously have no fat reserves and can quickly starve if they do not locate food. Less than a week after beginning life as a single fertilized cell, the tiny fish begins to hunt for food. The larva has large eyes and can detect moving prey, often single-celled protozoans such as *Paramecium*. As it grows, the larva graduates to larger, more substantial food, including tiny aquatic worms

Above: A three-day-old zebra pleco fry is still heavily reliant on its yolk sac for food.

and crustaceans. The larva must feed almost continuously to supply the energy demands of its growing body. Many succumb to starvation at this stage, unable to fuel the furnace within. Unlike their parents, larval fish tend to have a continuous fin that extends around the rear half of the body, rather like a frog tadpole. One reason for this is to counteract the density of water, which is 800 times denser than air. For a larval fish with its newly formed muscles, swimming in this viscous environment must be exhausting.

Left: This mass of "wrigglers" (Boulenger-ochromis microlepis fry) will soon use up their reserves and need to begin hunting.

Q: How does a larval fish sense its world?

A: The crucially important, complex sensory systems are in the final stages of development during the larval stage. However, the connections between the larva's nervous system and the motor cells that control movement, are still incomplete. This is why if you touch a newly hatched larva it does not dart away. Larval fish tend to have huge eyes – a clue to the importance of their sense of sight at this point in their development. Gradually, as the fish is "wired up," its senses and its movement become co-ordinated and it becomes better able not only to hunt but also to avoid its predators.

Below: Free-swimming fry feed voraciously on brine shrimp nauplii. They must feed almost constantly during their early life.

Juvenile fish

Early in its life, a fish makes the transformation from larva to juvenile; for the first time in its life, it now looks like a miniature version of its own parents. This change is sometimes described as a metamorphosis, although the changes that occur in fish at this time are less dramatic than those seen in caterpillars or tadpoles. Nonetheless, important changes do occur: the fish develops pigmentation and the continuous fin that surrounded the hind part of its body breaks down into distinct dorsal, caudal, anal, and pelvic fins. The body changes shape, from the tiny, glasslike sliver typical of larvae of all species, to a recognizable member of its own.

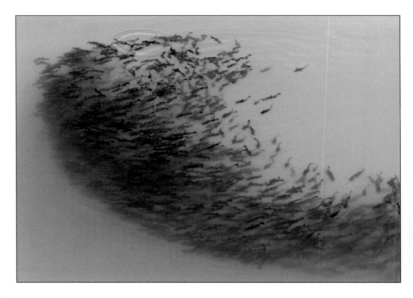

Above: A swarm of young black bullhead catfish (Ameiurus melas) gather to feed in surface waters.

Q: What drives juvenile fish behavior?

A: Staying alive is obviously the most important motivation, but as well as dodging predators, juvenile fish need to feed voraciously in order to grow. Each extra millimeter can mean one less predator to worry about. Even though foraging exposes juvenile fish to risk, staying safe at home is not necessarily an option, because small animals have fewer fat reserves than larger individuals and must feed regularly.

Q: Do different fish use different strategies?

A: Solving the problem of balancing the benefits of extra feeding against the risk of coming face to face with a predator varies between individuals. The extent to which individual fish can differ may come as a surprise. Recent research has shown how, in a given situation, some individuals will consistently adopt a "high-risk, high-reward" strategy, while others are far more cautious, taking more of a "safety-first" viewpoint. These different personality types have become known as "bold" and "shy" respectively. Research on zebra danios (Danio rerio), for instance, has shown that bold individuals will accept something like ten times the level of risk for a particular reward compared to shy fish. The gamble taken by bold fish is that in exposing themselves to this risk they will grow far more rapidly than their shy counterparts, reaching adulthood and the all-important finishing line – reproducing for themselves - sooner. Shy individuals keep out of harm's way and grow slowly, although their ultimate goal is the same. The difference between bold and shy fish can be easily seen in the aquarium; some bolder fish will consistently be first to the food. In addition, some will recover their normal behavior patterns more quickly than others after being introduced to a new tank.

Below: Levels of aggression are typically lower in juvenile groups than between adults.

Right: During their early life, fish like these Boulengerochromis microlepis *gather together into tight groups for safety.*

Q: How do juvenile fish stay out of trouble?

A: Juvenile fish have a number of ways to reduce the risks that go with being small in a dangerous world. One obvious example is in juvenile coloration – younger fish sometimes have different, less showy patterns than adults. Juvenile rainbowfish, for example, are often very plain by comparison to the dramatic adult hues, and male guppies do not exhibit their showy color patterns until they reach maturity. Another example is the way in which some fish, such as cichlids, school as youngsters, benefiting from the protection that schooling provides, before leaving the group to establish their own territories when they become adults.

Adult fish

Only a tiny percentage of fish reach adulthood; most either starve or become food themselves. Those that survive this long do so by a combination of good luck and good genes. Having reached sexual maturity, they now have the chance to pass on those successful genes to their own offspring.

Q: When does a juvenile fish become an adult?

A: The transition from juvenile to adult comes when the fish reaches sexual maturity. Its appearance changes; males and females become easier to tell apart and often advertise their maturity through color patterns. Breeding adults are often far more colorful than juveniles, and adult males are very often more colorful than adult females. But as adulthood can change the way that fishes look, it also changes the way they behave. As juveniles, fishes' main concerns were to find food and avoid predators; once they reach adulthood, reproduction goes straight to the top of their list. As a result, fish may often become more aggressive as they seek to stake their claim, especially with members of their own sex, who are now competitors for breeding opportunities. They may also start to defend territories and attempt to court potential mates.

Q: What changes when a fish becomes an adult?

A: As juveniles, fish use most of their energy to grow. Once they reach adulthood this energy is switched to producing eggs or sperm and growth slows. Female livebearers, such as swordtails (*Xiphophorus helleri*), can reach

Left: The onset of maturity is often accompanied by several obvious changes in physical appearance in many fish species, such as the hump on the head of this mature male Cyphotilapia frontosa.

Left: Annual growth rings can be clearly seen on this magnified image of a fish scale.

Q: What is old for a fish?

A: Fish in the wild seldom die of old age. This may be because they have been caught by predators – an ever-present risk – or parasites or simply that the wear and tear of everyday life – raising young and fighting rivals – has weakened them, perhaps fatally. For example, an extensive study on cichlids in Lake Tanganyika showed their average age to be three years and the oldest to be 10. However, there are records of these same species reaching over 20 years of age in the aquarium. The age at which fish can be considered old varies from species to species. Fish such as guppies and African killifish would be lucky to attain 12 months, whereas some of the larger catfish and cyprinids can continue for two or three decades.

considerable sizes if they remain unmated. If they start to reproduce as soon as they become mature, they may only reach half the size. Larger females produce more offspring, so it can be beneficial for an individual to delay breeding. Alternatively, if there are many predators in the environment, prey fish sometimes respond by breeding at younger ages. This phenomenon is seen in guppy populations: those that live alongside pike cichlids and blue acaras reach maturity considerably earlier than those that live in predator-free populations.

Q: Do fish ever stop growing?

A: Fish continue to grow throughout their lives, although their rate of growth slows with every passing year. It is for this reason that biologists are able to determine the age of fish by counting rings on the scales or, for greater accuracy, doing the same using the fish's earbone, the otolith. A fish's age can also be estimated from its appearance: as fish get older, their muscles tighten and this can be seen in the way that superannuated fish often have characteristic curved spines.

Below: Older fish are slower to recover from injury and can sometimes develop a curved spine.

Chapter 4
Finding food

All animals must feed in order to maintain an energy supply to fuel their metabolic processes. Each individual faces competition for scarce food resources, and only those that are consistently successful are able to grow and reproduce.

Finding sufficient food is not just about being able to fight for a share when rich pickings are on offer; it is also about innovating and diversifying – trying new kinds of food and exploiting untapped resources. Over tens of thousands of years, fish have evolved to be expert foragers, feeding on a huge range of different food sources, both animal and vegetable. Some specialize on a particular kind of food, others are opportunists, feeding on whatever they can. One thing all species have in common is that they are experts in spotting an opportunity and hunting out their next meal.

Q: Where do different fish species find their food?

A: Fish use a variety of techniques when foraging. They can either seek out their prey or they can lie in ambush and wait

for it to come to them. If they look for their own food, they often visit rich feeding grounds where their chances of success will be much greater. Fish in rivers often rely on the current to provide them with food. Food particles, including fly larvae that have been dislodged by the current or the fry of other fishes, are unable to negotiate the flow and so drift downstream to be

Above: Fish are adept at finding food wherever it may be hidden. Here a Lethrinops lethrinus *searches the substrate for food.*

met by eager hunters. In lakes, shallow waters are particularly rich in food, perhaps because they contain weed beds that harbor small prey animals. For herbivores, the substrate in these areas is often bathed in sunshine and the

algae grows rapidly here. Another means of finding food is to sniff it out – fish have an excellent sense of smell and use it to home in on their food. If they pick up the faint odor of a prey animal, they are often able to follow the trail back to its source and feast on whatever awaits them there.

Q: *How do fish forage effectively?*

A: Quite naturally, many of the animals that are the preferred prey of fishes hide. Some, such as water fleas *(Daphnia* sp.*)*, even respond to exposure to fish by developing different shapes, including growing spiky projections that make it more difficult for fish to handle them. But as fast as their prey work out ways to keep themselves out of harm's way, fish find a means to overcome the problem. Often when fish try a novel and difficult type of prey, they are not especially efficient at dealing with it. But practice makes perfect and fish have shown themselves to be experts at learning new tricks. Researchers looking at how quickly fish can learn have shown that most species can go from novice to expert in their dealings with an unusual food in as few as five attempts. Some species hunt more actively, fanning the bottom substrate with their pectoral fins to expose hidden prey, others dig down for the same reason. Some cichlids actually turn over small rocks and pebbles to find the animals hidden beneath.

Below: The different diets of fish are reflected in their widely differing mouth structures. Each is adapted to its own feeding niche.

Fish diets in the wild

In their natural habitats, the majority of tropical aquarium fishes are opportunists, or generalist feeders. If they come across a tempting morsel, they investigate it, often by mouthing it; if it is edible they will eat it, if not they will eject it, spitting it back out of their mouths. In this way, they sample a huge variety of potential foods, learning what is and what is not food. As a result, wild fish often have an incredibly diverse diet.

Q: *What's a typical wild diet for a fish such as a tetra?*

A: With its iridescent blue and vivid red colors, the cardinal tetra is one of the most striking fishes in the world. Huge numbers are collected and exported each year from their Amazonian home, but although they are a familiar sight in aquarium shops, little is known of their life in the wild. One of the most important steps in finding out about the biology of any species is to find out what it eats.

Researchers examining the diet of cardinal tetras from flooded forests and stream tributaries of the Rio Negro found that the fish were naturally eating a very broad range of foods. The stomach contents of the fish included crustaceans, such as *Daphnia* species and copepods, the larvae and adults of flies, mosquitoes, beetles, and bugs, as well as ants,

Below: Cichlids crop the algae and pick off tiny invertebrates from the rocks along the shores of Lake Malawi.

Left: Fishes specializing in different diets throughout their lifetime can sometimes develop slightly different appearances, known as morphotypes. These are two morphotypes of the cichlid Herichthys minckleyi *in the wild in Mexico.*

shrimps, fish fry, eggs, algae, and fibrous plant matter. The smaller fish – those measuring 1 inch (1 to 1.5 cm) – also preyed extensively on tiny rotifers. Perhaps most surprisingly, the results also showed up scales and parts of other, larger fish, which suggests that the cardinal tetras are not averse to scavenging on dead fish.

Q: Do fish have favorite foods?

A: Just like us, individual fish often have their own preferences. For instance, they may become used to a select number of prey species. They learn where these are most likely to be found and

through practice become efficient at hunting and eating them. Quite often a change in diet can occur as a release from competition. If a large number of fish all compete for the same food resource, it can pay to switch to a new food type. This happens over and over again in nature, meaning that fish from the same species may specialize in different food. If evolution gets to work on this, it can produce two morphotypes, each of which is specialized in its own diet. (Morphotypes are members of the same species with different appearances.) The cichlid *Herichthys minckleyi* is an example of this. Two of these morphotypes coexist in their Central American home, one specializes in eating

molluscs, especially snails, the other typically snacks on larvae. Each eat their own favored prey far more efficiently than the other. Most interestingly of all, the two morphotypes look quite different from one another, as each has evolved characteristics that aid their diet specialization, including different teeth and mouths.

Q: Do fish change behavior at feeding time?

A: Aquarists often notice how, when they add food, their fish go into a feeding frenzy. Their behavior switches from slow and placid to fast and frantic as they try to cram in as much food as possible before it disappears inside their tankmates. This feeding behavior also occurs in the wild when fish find a rich patch of food, where they take their cue from the feeding of others – "if they're eating it, I can too." Such observation helps fish to find their own next meal. However, the feeding frenzy is a dangerous time for the fish. They may be injured as they thrash around or very often they are themselves eaten by a predator taking advantage of their distraction as they feed.

Underwater eating

The importance of our hands for feeding ourselves is huge. We use them to catch food, to process it, and to carry it to our mouths, where we can hold it in place while we bite it. It may be obvious to point out that fish lack arms, yet this does not inhibit them! Fish also differ from humans in that while we chew our food, eating it a bite at a time, fish usually eat their prey in one go, with very little chewing. To complicate matters further for fish, they often eat other live animals, which usually did not plan to feature on the menu, and that try to make things as difficult as possible for their predator.

Q: *How do fish overcome the problem of getting hold of their prey?*

A: The solution for many fish is to vacuum up their food. By opening their mouths and expanding their buccal cavity, fish create an area of low pressure and water rushes in from outside to equalize this. If they manage to time it just right, their hapless prey is also impelled into their mouths. When the fish close their mouths, the food is trapped there when the excess water is pushed out of the gills. Fish, especially those that eat other fish, have extraordinarily large mouths, enabling them to produce a powerful suction current and to accommodate

large prey items when they catch them.

Q: *Do fish have teeth?*

A: Teeth are an essential part of a fish's foraging toolbox and an amazingly wide variety of types and shapes exist between species, each adapted to that species' particular diet. Generalist fish, such as tiger barbs, often have simple peglike teeth that can grab and hold pretty much anything. Specialists, like Chinese algae-eaters, have flatter teeth for rasping at algae, whereas fish predators have wickedly sharp, backward-pointing teeth that efficiently trap struggling prey. Fish do not only have teeth in their

Sucking up a meal

The demands of living under water are very different from those we experience on dry land. One particular problem is how to get unwilling prey into your mouth!

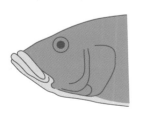

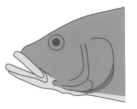

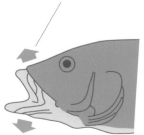

The predator rapidly opens its mouth, everting its jaws and pushing them towards its prey.

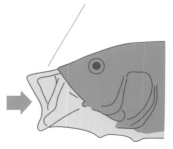

The sudden increase in volume creates a vacuum in the fish's mouth and water rushes in.

Above: Many fish have simple peglike teeth like this to help them maintain their grip on living prey and prevent its escape.

Q: How much food can fish eat?

A: In an unpredictable world, it can often pay fish to jam themselves with food whenever possible; who knows when the next meal might come along, especially if you are a predator. Consequently, fish can expand their stomachs far more than humans. Certain species can accommodate enormous meals – out-and-out predators can often tackle prey that is half their own size – and their whole bodies become distended. However, as the food is broken down, the fish revert back to their typical shape. They store fat in a totally different way to humans and, as a result, do not usually look podgy.

jaws, like us. They very often also have pharyngeal teeth in the roof of the mouth, and specialized tongues, both of which provide extra grip.

Right: As well as everting their mouths during feeding, fish sometimes "yawn," presumably to keep the mouth in top condition.

Capturing food

The greatest problem with eating under water is getting hold of the food. As a simple test, try pushing your finger towards something small, such as a cichlid pellet. All being well, you should make a good contact. In fact, you should be able to push the pellet along quite easily for a distance. Now try the same, but with the pellet in a tub of water. It is far more difficult, because as your finger moves along, it pushes a wave of pressure along in front of it which knocks the pellet to one side. To counteract this, fish feed in an ingenious way.

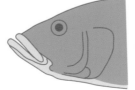

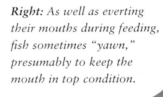

Feeding at the substrate

The bottom sediments of aquatic habitats are rich in decaying organic matter from both plant leaves and stems and the bodies of everything from plankton to fish. These sediments are home to countless small invertebrate animals, themselves feeding on the sediments or hiding among them. Although sometimes thought of as nothing more than dirt by aquarists, this detritus and the animals it contains represent one of the most concentrated food resources available to fish. Many species use it and some, known as detritivores, specialize in extracting food from it.

Q: Can fish really eat dirt?

A: Analysis of many species' diets has revealed that detritus plays a major part in fish nutrition. Detritivory is especially common during the low-water season of many tropical rivers, including the Orinoco and Zambezi, when alternative foods become progressively harder to find. At these times of year, the edible sediments consist mostly of decaying plant matter. Although it sounds unappetizing, this still has a reasonable amount of value as a food, not only for the vegetable matter, but also for the community of tiny protozoans such as *Paramecium* that live on it. Even during more plentiful times of year, detritus still forms a significant part of the diet of omnivorous fish.

Q: How are fish adapted to feeding from the substrate?

A: Detritivores are extremely common in tropical systems and the way they turn over and recycle the nutrient has a major effect on the ecosystems they live in. Not only that, but these fish form the prey of larger fish, so a whole food web is connected by these vital creatures. Although few of the major detritivores of the Amazon have found popularity in the aquarium trade, a large number of omnivorous species that sift the detritus are commonly found, including the *Corydoras* group of catfish and *Geophagus* cichlids, whose name translates as "earth-eaters." Fish that feed at the substrate tend to have mouths at the end of their snouts, very often positioned low down on the head, or even beneath it. Often, the eyes of

Below: Scleromystax barbatus *sifting through the sand at the substrate, filtering out small morsels of food as it does so.*

Above: Geophagus steindachneri *is typical of the so-called earth-eaters in that its mouth is ventrally positioned for substrate feeding.*

these fish are set back, away from the mouth, which prevents them from being damaged as the fish digs for food. When feeding on detritus, fish take large quantities of food into their mouths and sift it, spitting out and discarding small stones and indigestible items. Often, the fish have a large number of tightly packed gill rakers, which act like a sieve, allowing the water through, but catching the microscopic food particles before they escape.

Q: If detritus is a natural part of aquatic ecosystems, why is it so essential to filter it from the home aquarium?

A: Sediments and detritus in the home aquarium can spell trouble for all the inhabitants because the decaying matter can

be a source of nitrites. What is more, it may appear unsightly. It is therefore understandable that aquariums are usually equipped with power filters to remove all hints of dirt before they have the chance to accumulate. However, it would be rewarding for anyone with a large aquarium to attempt a more naturalistic set-up, where low fish stocking densities allow for a filter-less system. Under these conditions, a layer of sediment would accumulate, feeding the plants and fish alike and creating a true aquatic ecosystem.

Fish mouths and gills

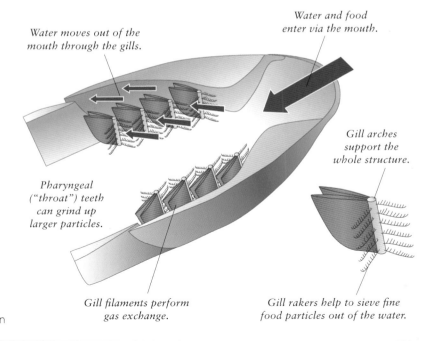

Water moves out of the mouth through the gills.

Water and food enter via the mouth.

Gill arches support the whole structure.

Pharyngeal ("throat") teeth can grind up larger particles.

Gill filaments perform gas exchange.

Gill rakers help to sieve fine food particles out of the water.

A spineless supper

What could be better than to snack on a spider or feast on a fly larva? You and I might disagree, but invertebrates of all kinds are the food of choice for countless fish species. They represent nutritious, bite-sized morsels for many aquarium fishes.

Q: How do invertebrates try to stay off the menu?

A: Being small and tasty is not an ideal strategy in the competitive underwater world. Consequently, invertebrates have evolved a wide range of defences against predation. Many, such as worms, hide; molluscs, including snails and mussels, put their stock in a protective shell; and crustaceans, such as *Daphnia*, grow spiky appendages when they detect the odor of fish in the water. But in each case the defence does not provide a total solution. Fish have evolved ways of overcoming these defences, although sometimes only specialists in a given kind of prey are consistently successful.

Right: Pencilfish are perfectly adapted for picking tiny animals from the water column.

Q: Do many fish eat plankton and other "midwater" animals?

A: Yes! Any small animal in the water column will be investigated by fish and eaten if it is bite-sized. The so-called water fleas (*Daphnia* spp.) and copepods are small relatives of crabs. They swim in the water column but can be difficult to catch, evading their hunters with bursts of speed. Often, they live in dense vegetation where they have a refuge from the attentions of most fishes. However, pencilfish possess the perfect narrow body for pursuing them into this aquatic undergrowth, and their small terminal mouths allow for accuracy in picking off their prey one by one.

Q: Why are mosquitofish so called?

A: It is estimated that mosquitoes have killed more humans by spreading malaria than any other animal. Man's response has been to introduce fish into the swamps and wetlands that act as nurseries for so many mosquitoes and biting flies in the tropics. Both the livebearing mosquitofish and guppies reproduce rapidly and were thought to have an

insatiable appetite for these larvae. However, recent studies of the diet of guppies in the wild show that algae makes up 75% of their intake and larvae only 24%. Thus their effectiveness is unproven and they often damage the indigenous aquatic animals as well. Nonetheless, larvae make excellent food, relying mainly on concealment to escape the fishes' attention. This strategy is often undermined by species such as mormyrids, which detect their presence electrically, and catfish, which explore the sediment using sensitive barbels.

Q: *Do any fish prey on snails?*

A: Aquatic habitats are rich in molluscs, and snails are especially common in fresh water. Their tough shells put them off-limits for most fishes, but a number of species specialize in overcoming this problem. Pufferfish have bony beaks with which to bite

Right: The fused, beaklike teeth of pufferfish make short work of snails and other molluscs. These fish can help to keep your aquarium clear of conical-shelled Malaysian livebearing snails.

open the snail shell, exposing the succulent flesh inside. The beaks grow continuously and without a tough diet to wear them down, overgrowth of the beak can prove a real problem in the aquarium. Doradid catfish also specialize in snails, as do

clown loaches (*Chromobotia macracanthus*) and a number of cichlids. In these cases, the fish have specialized, platelike pharyngeal teeth and powerful muscles that generate remarkable force to crush the snail shells.

A battery of small teeth help the fish to hold its prey.

Right: Catfish, such as this Synodontis petricola, *can detect tasty invertebrates hidden in the substrate.*

Flying food

Virtually all species of fish live their lives underwater. Those that do emerge, usually do so only for short spells and in these cases it is often to escape unforgiving conditions. For example, *Clarias* catfish escape from pools where the water level is dropping and both oxygen and food are scarce. Despite this, a large number of fish feed on terrestrial animals, especially flying insects, either picking them from the surface or leaping out to catch them – even shooting them down as they rest on overhanging leaves and branches.

Seeing above and below water

The Anableps eye is divided into two parts. It has an elliptical lens and two areas of retina used for vision above and below the water surface.

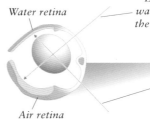

Water retina

Air retina

Light from above the water is focused through the short axis of the lens.

Light from below the water is focused through the long axis of the lens.

Left: Anableps anableps *(the four-eyed fish) is adapted to see everything that happens above and below the water surface.*

Q: Do fish benefit from the windfall of insects on the water surface?

A: Billions of insects every year are fatally attracted to rivers and lakes. Often, they may breed there and spend the early part of their lives underwater, but while water provides a nursery, it also claims huge numbers of adults. Should an insect blunder onto the water, the surface tension is often sufficient to overcome their feeble struggles. Huge numbers of flying insects die in this way,

but bad news for the flies is good news for the fish. They represent a rich food resource for fish and a number of species specialize in feeding at the water surface. Typically, these species have upturned – so-called "superior" – mouths sited towards the top of their heads. In addition, they tend to have fairly flat backs – ideal for cruising just below the water surface. The African butterflyfish *(Pantodon buchholzi)* is one such fish, lurking among floating vegetation, waiting to pounce on any insect unfortunate enough to drop onto the water surface.

Q: Do fish ever leave the water to feed?

A: The incredible four-eyed fish *(Anableps anableps)* is even more adept at this. It too lives at the water surface, but its uniquely positioned eyes allow it to see both above and below the water line simultaneously. In this way it can even ambush low-flying insects, leaping out of the water to snatch them on the wing. In fact, most surface-feeders are capable of jumping from the water to take prey, but the silver arowana *(Osteoglossum* *bicirrhosum)* has developed these skills to a remarkable extent. Large individuals, measuring up to 3 feet (1 m) long, can jump considerable distances out of the water to snatch unwary insects and even small birds from overhanging vegetation in their Amazonian home. They accelerate from deeper water, only opening their mouths fully after clearing the surface, thereby reducing drag. The comparatively large mouths of arowanas allow them to take a variety of prey in this way – there are even claims of small monkeys being on the menu.

Q: *How do archerfish capture their prey?*

A: When it comes to solving the problem of feeding on flying insects, the prize for innovation must go to the archerfish, which is found in estuaries and brackish water regions across Asia. Archerfish capture their prey by shooting them down with rapid and precise drops of water. They are able to spit the water to heights of up 4 feet (1.2 m) above the surface, giving them a huge range. The pressure needed to achieve this is generated by the tongue, while grooves in the mouth serve to direct the shot. The fish are capable of amazing accuracy, especially over shorter distances. There are stories of some individuals who would shoot and put out their owners' cigarettes if they approached the tank, although whether this was for health reasons or because they mistook them for glow-worms is not known!

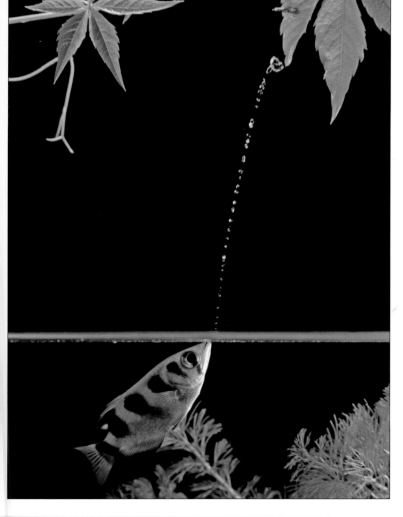

Left: The archerfish (Toxotes jaculatrix) *has evolved a unique solution to a lack of insect food in the waters of its habitat.*

Fish predators of eggs and fry

It's a tough life being a fish, especially a young fish. Everything, but everything, can and will eat you. The prospects for a newly fertilized egg are grim. Survivorship for these eggs to adulthood can be as low as a fraction of 1%. Most of the mortality occurs in the first few days of life. Each week that a fish fry survives represents a huge step towards its ultimate survival. Danger lurks at every corner and much of it comes from a highly unexpected direction.

Q: *Do fish ever turn cannibal?*

A: Although the image of an out-and-out predator such as a wolf fish (*Hoplias malabaricus*) may spring to mind when we imagine the risks that fish face, very often their greatest enemies are larger individuals of their own species. From the outset, when fish spawn, the eggs are greedily gobbled up by any fish in the area, and for good reason: they offer excellent nourishment. Newly hatched fry hardly fare any better; they are eaten by nearly everything, including their own parents, in some cases.

Researchers in Nicaragua found that the largest single predator of convict cichlid fry were subadult convict cichlids themselves. Again, this makes sense. When fish eat, their bodies break down the food and, put simply, convert the food into the building blocks that they need to grow or maintain their own bodies. Eating conspecifics means that every necessary nutrient is present and in the correct proportions. For fishkeepers, seeing a livebearer such as a black molly (*Poecilia sphenops*) giving birth in the home aquarium can be quite harrowing,

as the newly born offspring are rapidly chased down and eaten by the other tank inhabitants and sometimes, even their own mother. Although hard for us to understand, fish seem to eat their own fry when they assess that their chances of survival are slim – "if the kids are going to be eaten anyway, I might as well eat them myself." This recycling allows

Below: Discus eggs such as these laid on an exposed branch have to be diligently defended by their parents – plenty of opportunists will take a risk for food.

the parents to recover some of the huge energetic expenditure of parenthood, preparing them for their next effort, when perhaps conditions will be better.

Q: How do fish sense that eggs may be on the menu?

A: Just as the smell of our favorite food being prepared can cause us to hang around the kitchen, so the smell of hormones in the water during a breeding season can produce a similar effect in fishes. The ability of fishes to detect minute concentrations of chemicals in the water means that the smell of spawning draws eager predators from all around. The only defense that fish can muster is to produce a huge number of eggs – more than the predators can eat at once – and

to scatter them widely or to guard them (see page 166). Even so, the smell of eggs is a powerful stimulant for fish and the promise of rich, defenseless pickings is often just too good to miss.

Above: Few fish pass up the chance to eat the eggs of another species. Here Telmatochromis brichardi *feeds at an unguarded nest.*

Below: Very few fish survive to adulthood. This juvenile Dimidiochromis *has been captured by a patrolling* Buccochromis.

Predators of adult fish

The food web in the aquatic environment is topped by hunters, fish that hunt and kill other fish. Fish are a good food in terms of nutrition but they have a major drawback – they are slippery customers and difficult to catch. The secret of success for piscivorous (fish-eating) fish is to get as close as possible to the intended prey without being detected before launching an attack. To enable these hunters to do this, they have adopted a variety of cunning strategies.

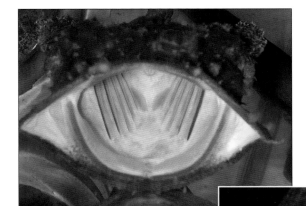

Left: *The huge mouth of this catfish* (Chaca chaca) *is the last thing many small fish will see.*

Q: *How do predatory fish avoid scaring their prey?*

A: One way to get to within striking distance is to blend into the background and be very, very patient. Wide-mouthed catfish (*Chaca chaca*) conceal themselves in the substrate, often with only their eyes betraying their presence, and then play a waiting game. If a small fish happens to stray too close, the catfish erupts out of its hiding place and engulfs its unfortunate prey. Leaf fish (*Monocirrhus polyacanthus*) perform a similar trick. As their name suggests, they are masters

of disguise. Resembling a fallen leaf, they bide their time among the vegetation until a fish makes its final mistake and approaches too close.

Q: *What are the main features of an ambush predator?*

A: Predators that ambush their victims by speeding from concealment often share a common body plan: large head, long, tapered body, and fins set towards the back of the fish, providing a huge amount of acceleration from a hiding place. Ambush predators have a large amount of white, anaerobic, fast-twitch muscle, just like human

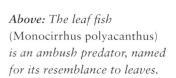

Above: *The leaf fish* (Monocirrhus polyacanthus) *is an ambush predator, named for its resemblance to leaves.*

Above: The mouth of the pike livebearer (Belonesox belizanus) *bristles with teeth – there can be no escape for prey once caught.*

sprinters. When it comes to making a quick start, these fish have no equal. Lastly, they have extremely large mouths, often lined with forbidding, backward-pointing teeth. This body design can be seen across a range of completely unrelated piscivores – pike cichlids *(Crenicichla* spp.*)*, pike livebearers *(Belonesox belizanus),* and pike characins *(Phago spp., Luciocharax* spp.*, Hydrocinus* spp.*)*. Although such fish rely mainly on prey fish swimming past their place of concealment, they also stalk their quarry, moving extremely stealthily, almost imperceptibly closer, with barely a ripple of their fins, until they come within range of their target.

Q: Can fish stalk their prey?

A: Large nocturnal predators, including many members of the catfish family, stalk their prey in the dark. Recent research has shown that the hunters follow the vortices left behind by a passing fish, approaching closer and closer

Below: At night, catfish such as this spotted catfish (Pimelodus pictus) *emerge to hunt resting prey.*

until they can attack. Other species rely on less subtle techniques; spotted catfish *(Pimelodus pictus)* chase their targets (usually any fish small enough to fit into their mouths) to exhaustion.

Q: Do predators make good aquarium fish?

A: Maintaining piscivores in the home aquarium can be difficult for a variety of reasons. Many predators are strangely skittish and fail to settle. Furthermore, fish such as the pike livebearer are confirmed piscivores and need to be fed with live fish. Although this is perfectly natural behavior – predation is a fact of life for fishes – many fishkeepers may feel uncomfortable breeding guppies to feed to a predator. If this is the case, the aquarist should think hard before acquiring such a fish.

Herbivores – catfish

Although almost absent from temperate waters, there is a huge diversity of catfishes in the lakes and rivers of the tropics. Their diet is just as diverse as the catfish themselves, but among them is a large group of specialist algae-eaters. These include a number of long-standing aquarium favorites, particularly members of the Loricariidae family such as the pleco (*Hypostomus plecostomus*), the bristlenose catfish (*Ancistrus ancistrus*), and the whiptail catfishes. All are incredibly well adapted for their life of rasping off the rich algal film that forms on fallen wood and stones.

Q: *How are the algae-eating catfishes adapted for their grazing lifestyle?*

A: Perhaps the most remarkable feature of these fish is the mouth. In each case, it is positioned ventrally, beneath the fish's body. The belly is flat, creating a highly streamlined profile. This is an advantage for fish that move along the substrate in their home waters, which in many cases are fast-flowing streams. But it is not just their hydrodynamic shape that allows these catfish to prosper in whitewater habitats. Their mouths also provide powerful suction, fitting snugly and forming a seal on the surface that they feed from. While the fleshy lobes of their mouths do the holding, highly adapted jaws rasp at their holdfast. The teeth vary between species: those that eat soft algae, including *Ancistrus* sp., have broad flat teeth, whereas *Panaque* sp. have spoon-shaped teeth that enable them to gouge tougher substances, such as fallen wood.

Q: *Is the catfish's armor enough on its own to protect the fish?*

A: Although many catfish carry armored plates on their back and flanks to protect them from attack (see page 112), fish such as the whiptailed catfish are also extremely well camouflaged.

Scraping a living

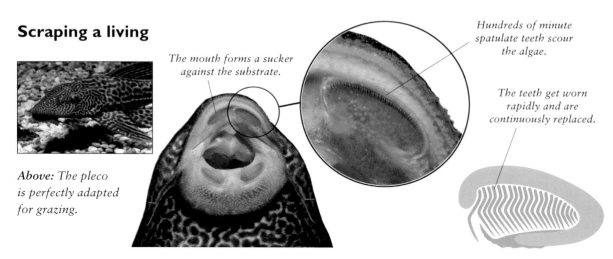

The mouth forms a sucker against the substrate.

Hundreds of minute spatulate teeth scour the algae.

The teeth get worn rapidly and are continuously replaced.

Above: *The pleco is perfectly adapted for grazing.*

Above: The Chinese algae-eater (Gyrinocheilus aymonieri) fills the same feeding niche as the South American pleco.

As they feed on roots and the submerged branches of trees, they blend perfectly into their environment because their elongated bodies resemble the twigs that surround them.

Q: So are these fish almost like vacuum cleaners for the home aquarium?

A: Although it tends to live in still or slowly flowing waters, the Chinese algae-eater *(Gyrinocheilus aymonieri)* fills a niche similar to the armoured catfish of Africa and South America. It is often bought as a scavenger for the community aquarium at home because it is cheap and believed to remain much smaller than the tank-busting plecs. Of course, the reality is that sucking loaches are not scavengers, but algae-eaters. What is more, they can grow to an impressive size – some reaching 10 inches (25 cm). Added to this, they are occasionally known to graze on the sides of their tankmates – the mucus presumably making a change from the regular diet of greens. The solution for algae in an aquarium is balance: efficient filtration to remove excess nitrates, a sensible light regime and no direct sunlight. The various kinds of algae-eaters deserve a place in the aquarium in their own right, not just to work as a maintenance team.

Q: How do algae-eaters distribute themselves to get the most food?

A: Grazing animals, such as the plec, live in a world where food is everywhere, because algae takes hold wherever a surface faces the sun. Nevertheless, their food is only spread thinly, so the fish distribute themselves carefully, going where the food is. More than this, they seek an area where they can obtain the most food with the least amount of competition. It is pointless simply to go where the richest algal mat is, if that means constantly fighting off others. A study on plecs in their Amazon home showed that although there were fewer fish in the deeper waters where the algae is not as rich, neither were they all crowded into the shallow pools at the margins where the algae is at its most succulent. Instead, the fish distributed themselves perfectly throughout their environment so that each maximized its food intake.

Herbivores – cichlids

The bright sunshine of the tropics is great news for the group of microscopic plants called algae. They prosper, especially in shallow waters, and because they photosynthesize, they produce sugars that attract herbivores to feast on them. Many species of algae grow as a covering on underwater substrates, but others, such as diatoms and *Volvox* sp., live freely in the water column. Fishes can eat both types and some have become highly specialized to reap this rich harvest.

Q: *Can fish ever take advantage of the algal blooms that form in some aquatic habitats?*

A: Pond owners are only too well aware that under certain conditions, especially in the summer months, their pools can turn into green soups. The organisms behind this phenomenon are algae, or more correctly, phytoplankton. Millions upon millions of these microscopic, single-celled plants contribute to this bloom yet very few fish are capable of taking direct advantage of it.

Nonetheless, the algae, which are at the bottom of the food chain, feed animals such as *Daphnia*, whose consequent rocketing numbers add up to a boon for the fish. One group of fish that do take advantage of the phytoplankton are the Tilapines. These cichlids collect the algae from the water using their finely meshed gillrakers and specially secreted mucus to trap and collect them, almost like a spider's web.

Q: *I've noticed that Rift Lake cichlids often graze on the rocks. What are they eating?*

A: The waters of Lake Malawi contain a large number of cichlid species that graze on the algae

Above: The mouths of fish reflect their diet. It is thought that Labeotropheus fuelleborni *uses its snout to lever algae from rocks.*

covering the rocks. Whether these species should really be regarded as herbivores is a matter for debate. The reason for this is that the film of algae is also home to a huge number of tiny creatures such as ostracods, fly larvae, and copepods. One survey estimated that as many as 300,000 of these animals could be found in 4 square miles (1 m^2) of algae-coated rock surface. This tasty mix of animal and vegetable matter, sometimes referred to as "aufwuchs" in the literature, is a superb and rapidly replenishing source of food for a number of mbuna. One species

that specialises on this food is the cichlid *Labeotropheus fuelleborni*. Its distinguishing feature is a fleshy snout, which it is thought may act as a lever when the fish is cropping hair algae from the rocks. The ventrally situated mouth allows it to feed parallel to the rocks in extremely shallow waters, which are out of range for those fish with terminal mouths.

Below: Algae is not always grazed from hard surfaces – some species filter algae suspended in the water.

They have to stand on end to bite at the algae, and have lines of teeth inside the mouth that act like a file to rasp the aufwuchs from the rocks.

Q: Do many fish eat plant leaves, or do they just graze their surfaces?

A: Some haplochromine cichlids take the algae from the plants directly, cleaning the leaves without damaging them. Other species of fish pass up the algae

and instead feed on the plants themselves. The problem with this is that plants are generally tougher than algae so the fish have powerful jaws with slicing teeth that bite pieces out of the plant. Silver dollars (*Metynnis* spp. – not cichlids, but characins) specialize in this and can reduce aquatic plants to a few sorry shreds in record time. A school of these in the home aquarium is a beautiful sight but your aquascaping options are restricted to plastic plants.

Piranha and pacu

While the majority of fish species concentrate their efforts on bite-sized invertebrates, small fish or plant matter, there are other options for the more adventurous piscine diners. This is exemplified by two very closely related South American characins, the red-bellied piranha *(Pygocentrus nattereri)* and the tambacqui, or pacu *(Colossoma* spp.), which pursue two unusual and highly specialized diet plans.

Q: How deadly are piranhas?

A: The infamous piranha was first brought to popular attention in the early 20th century by the visit to Amazonia of then president, Theodore Roosevelt. Journalists covering his visit reported stories of horses being stripped to the bone in mere seconds by these voracious fish. The pressmen created a lasting image of a relentless and deadly predator that lurked in the mysterious forest rivers of Brazil. The truth, as ever, is rather more prosaic. For most of the year piranhas are relatively shy creatures, seldom attacking much

larger animals. Indeed, the children of the forest peoples bathe, swim, and splash in piranha-infested waters without harm. But there is a central grain of truth to the early reports of the piranha's flesh-shredding activities. During the dry season the fish are constrained to live in small and

shrinking pools. Food at these times is in extremely short supply and the fish are far more likely to attack, especially if their victim – often a large aquatic rodent such as a coypu – is injured. Once the smell of blood is in the water, the excited fish go into a feeding frenzy, tearing at their victim and,

Above: The piranha is found not only in the main rivers, but also in back-water streams such as this, where prey may be cornered.

Right: The fierce dentition of the piranha helped to spread its dramatic reputation as a man-eater, which is largely undeserved.

Right: Pacu can grow to considerable sizes on their vegetarian diet of tough seeds, fruits, and nuts.

sometimes, at each other. Piranhas also often gather beneath the nests of storks and similar birds, waiting for the fledging youngsters to make a mistake and fall into the water.

Q: So what's so unusual about piranhas?

A: Plenty of fish eat flesh of one kind or another, but piranhas are exceptional in the way they take bites out of larger animals. Most fish only attack prey that they can swallow whole. Piranhas are equipped with a mouthful of large, razor-sharp teeth that enable them to slice almost surgically through skin, flesh, and cartilage and remove a chunk. The

second unusual aspect of piranha behaviour is that, unlike almost all major predators, they live in schools. This is likely to be as a result of the distribution of their food. It also means that during a feeding frenzy, any individual that is not quick enough to seize a mouthful and retire may be itself targeted in error by its schoolmates, resulting in serious injuries, even death.

Q: Are there any vegetarian piranhas?

A: The pacu is a close relative of the piranha and shares its deep, round body, but unlike its cousin, it is a vegetarian. Even the young fish, which are carried

along with the other river fish onto the forested floodplains during the rains, eat grass seeds. As they grow, they graduate to the fruits, nuts, and seeds shed by the trees and which float on the water surface. Pacu have immensely powerful jaws and molarlike teeth that enable them to crush tough seed casings and nut shells and to access food that no other fish can. Interestingly, this process often does not kill the seed but rather activates it, and its passage through the fish's digestive system triggers germination. As a result, pacu are important distributors of plant seeds throughout the flooded forest in their native home.

Specialist feeders

Whereas most fishes tend to choose their food from within the same broad range of invertebrates, small fish, and vegetable matter, a significant minority have rather more unusual tastes. This kind of diet specialization is most commonly seen in habitats where a large number of species compete for the same kinds of food. By diversifying their diet into new and unexploited areas, they gain what is known as competitive release.

Homing in on a ho

Most fish tend to pick on smaller prey, but the blood-sucking candhiru and its relatives do the opposite, seeking out larger fish to feed on.

Fish naturally emit waste ammonia and urea from the gills.

The candhiru follows this trail to the source.

Q: Are there any truly parasitic fish?

A: Parasites are animals that obtain their food from another, usually larger, animal species, but "ideally" without killing them. Nearly all parasite species are invertebrates – animals without backbones, such as ticks and tapeworms. But in the Amazon there are fish that have adopted this lifestyle with considerable success. The infamous candhiru is a tiny catfish, seldom more than 2 inches (6 cm) long, that seeks out its victims by following the traces of urea that they emit from their gills as they breathe and excrete.

Once it picks up an odor trail, it follows it to the source and slips inside the gill cover. It then locks itself in place with specialized crampon-like spines on its gill covers, bites into the rich blood vessels of its host's gills and settles down to a blood meal. Once it has drunk its fill, it leaves its host and retires to the safety of the leaf litter at the bottom of the river, where it can contentedly digest. The way the candhiru finds its food – using urea trails – means that it can sometimes mistakenly follow trails produced by bathing mammals, including people, if they should urinate into the water. If this happens, and the candhiru swims

Right: Eye-biter or basic predator? Either way, Dimidiochromis compressiceps is extremely laterally compressed, making it impossible for prey to see it head-on.

somewhere it should not, the consequences for both the fish and the bather are serious.

Q: *Do fish have other unusual diets?*

A: A number of fish species, including representatives of the catfish and cichlid families, have evolved the habit of dining out on the scales of other species. Where there are plenty of fish about this is a clever ploy – scales are rich in protein and can be nipped from their owners fairly simply with the right dental

Above: In the wild, the Lake Malawi cichlid Docimodus evelynae *feeds on the skin of catfish.*

tool kit. Some scale-eaters have evolved color patterns that mimic those of their hosts. This allows them to mix with them almost like "wolves in sheep's clothing," only revealing their gory intent at the last minute. Others feed obligately (meaning that this is their sole food source) on the mucus of various fish species. Mucus protects fish from infections and contains

protein compounds, so once again, this is a pretty good diet if there are enough fish around.

Q: *Does the infamous eye-biter cichlid really live up to its name?*

A: Some species, including *Dimidiochromis compressiceps,* are famed for another gruesome habit, that of eating the eyes from their living victims. Although this is quite conceivable, there is a lack of hard evidence to support the idea. Even if eye-biting is just a rare dietary excursion, it is clear that in fish-rich communities only a tiny number of fish species may feed by taking the body tissues of others, whether it be fins, scales, mucus, or eyes. Hands up anyone who still thinks it's easy being a fish!

Chapter 5
Staying alive

The outlook for a newly hatched or newborn fish is bleak. The probability of the young surviving to adulthood is tiny; most will suffer the fate of being eaten. Their predators lurk everywhere, above and below the water, and come in every guise.

Fry are at risk from the deadly tentacles of the hydra and the jaws of a beetle larva, while a host of other fish, birds, and even animals such as snakes threaten them in later life. The dangers posed by birds to many fish is one reason why fish are so super-sensitive to any kind of movement passing over the top of the water. Most fish are defenseless – a soft parcel of valuable and tasty proteins and fats – which puts them at the top of the menu for many animals. The pressures they face are, therefore, very high.

Q: How does predation influence evolution in fishes?

A: Only fish that are successful in dodging predators have the chance to breed and to pass on their genes. Those characteristics that enabled the parent fish to survive are then passed on through their genes to their offspring and thus the process of evolution advances in tiny incremental steps. But while successive generations of prey fish become fractionally better able to avoid their predators, the predators respond in kind, producing an arms race of adaptation and counter-adaptation. And there are limits to how far the evolutionary process can take them; it can only work with the materials at hand. For instance, a neon tetra could not simply evolve large toxic spines. Even if it could, the costs of growing them and swimming while so encumbered would be disastrous.

Right: Most fish have adaptations to cope with danger, but few are as dramatic as those of the hatchetfish (Carnegiella spp.) which can take to the air and fly. The deep "keel" houses well-developed muscles to power their rapid escape strategy.

Q: How do fish defend themselves against predation?

A: Fishes' defenses against predation can occur at any stage in the so-called predation cycle. Some try to avoid detection by predators by using camouflage or by hiding. Others try to deter the predator from attacking by bluff, by being poisonous, or by their behavior. Some species have false eyespots that direct predators' attacks away from critical areas of the body. Most fish remain highly alert in the presence of predators, ready to dart away at speed. And if the worst comes to the worst, others have evolved armor and spines so that a predator is unlikely to be able to devour them. Here we will consider each strategy, looking at the incredible diversity of ways in which fish attempt to overcome their hunters.

Q: What has predation got to do with aquarium fish?

A: This is of course a book about aquarium fish and if all runs to plan, predation ought not to be a concern for domestic fish, should it? While this is true, fish in the home aquarium still display the behavior and appearance of their wild ancestors — what may be called the "ghost of predation past." Armored catfish are still armored and tetras still school. Although we do sometimes see a reduction in anti-predator behavior patterns in the home aquarium as each generation of fish raised in captivity become bolder, it often only takes a sudden fright to see their

Above: The vertical bars of angelfish help to break up their outline amid the vegetation, making them harder to see.

natural response come to the fore. Predation has had a huge influence on fish for millions of years and it will be a considerable while before the ghost of its effect disappears.

How not to be noticed

When predators are at large, it obviously pays to be inconspicuous. One way is to blend into the background, hoping to avoid detection by a hunter. Camouflage, or crypsis, is used widely by fish species for this purpose. A fish whose color matches its environment will live a great deal longer than one that stands out. Many species that are brightly colored as adults are comparatively plain as juveniles, adopting camouflage colors during the early stages of life for greater comparative safety. There are two main elements to blending in to the background: color matching and contour elimination.

Q: How do fish achieve camouflage in the natural world?

A: The extent to which fish match the colors in their environment varies between species. Some merely adopt a kind of drab overall color, whereas others have perfected the chameleon-like art of reacting and changing to their immediate surroundings, an ability known as adaptive camouflage.

Above: The transparent flesh of the glass catfish (Kryptopterus bicirrhis) *helps it to blend into its environment.*

This is most often seen among fishes that live on or near the substrate. Although marine flatfishes are the masters of this technique, many loaches and catfish are also highly adept. For fish that live in the main water column, such as penguinfish and silver dollars, silvery scales can reflect the light and colors of their underwater world. Some take this even further – Indian glassfish and glass catfish have silvery bellies but otherwise virtually transparent bodies, which act as camouflage by allowing the habitat's dominant colors to show right through them.

Q: How do fish maximize the benefits of camouflage?

A: For camouflage to be at its most effective, fish have to find ways of pulling off the trick of breaking up the outline and contours of their body. One common means of achieving this is by counter-shading. In this, the dorsal surface is dark in color and the belly is light, which allows the animal to blend in when seen from above against a deep background and from below when pictured against the sky. Another means of breaking up contours is known as disruptive coloration. Color pattern features such as stripes allow different parts of the body to blend into the background and break up its outline. Angelfish, tiger barbs

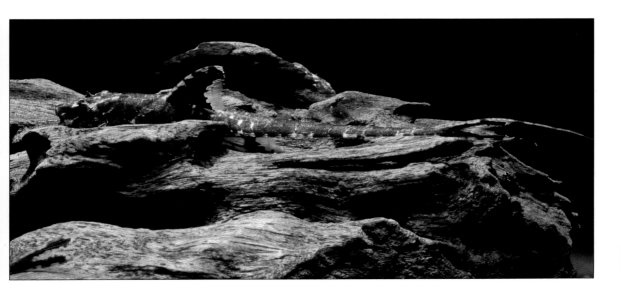

and kuhli loaches, among others, use this to good effect, especially against a background of vertical plant stems, such as reeds at the water's edge. A band across the face is also a common feature among fish, helping to break up the contrast and to hide the eye.

Q: Can predators use camouflage as well?

A: Camouflage is not only used to escape the notice of predators; it can be used by predators themselves to sneak inconspicuously to within striking distance of prey. The cichlid *Nimbochromis livingstonii* is a master of this; its mottled coloration provides excellent camouflage against

Above: This whiptail catfish (Rineloricaria lanceolata) merges perfectly into the wood that it rests and feeds on.

the substrate of Lake Malawi. This adaptation comes with an unusual accompanying behavior pattern: the fish "play dead" and lie on their sides against the bottom of the lake. This behavior,

which leads to their local name of "sleeper," combines with their cryptic coloration to help them escape the notice of both potential predators and prey.

Below: The mottled coloration of this Nimbochromis livingstonii, combined with its "dead" posture, help it to escape notice.

Hideouts

Fish can also avoid the attentions of their predators by hiding whenever danger threatens. They can do this either by seeking cover in the substrate or among rocks; or fleeing to places where their hunters cannot follow. For example, fish may choose to tough it out in an inhospitable environment, such as in the shallows or in places where there are low levels of dissolved oxygen. All these "hideouts" are correctly referred to as "refuges" and are of over-riding importance in the survival of vulnerable fish. Anyone whose livebearers have given birth in an unplanted aquarium will recognize this.

Q: How do fish decide when to hide and when to venture out?

A: Although the world is a dangerous place, especially for smaller fish, it is not an option to hide all the time; for one thing, hiding usually comes at the cost of missing out on feeding. So it pays to be selective and to respond only to immediate dangers; in the end, small fish

may outgrow many of their predators if they can keep feeding and increasing in size. In the wild, fish often live side by side with their predators. Schools of smaller species, such as barbs and tetras, are even likely to be in constant visual contact with larger, piscivorous hunters. Research has shown that fish are able to assess the danger that a predator poses, not only by its size and appearance, but also by more subtle cues. These include watching its behavior to see whether it is actively hunting and assessing chemical cues. Remarkably, these can tell fish

with a high degree of accuracy not only when a predator has fed but on what species. Prey fish show the greatest reactions to predators if they pick up the smell of their own species – it tells them whether the hunter has a taste for them. When this happens, prey fish stop eating and become super-alert, and if the cues become strong enough, they may seek a refuge.

Q: Who should hide?

A: The larger a fish grows, the safer it generally becomes. Small fish represent easy pickings

Assessing the risk

Fish in the wild usually live alongside, and in clear view of, their predators. They have a remarkable ability to work out levels of threat.

Prey fish are less cautious towards a predator that does not smell as though it has recently attacked their own kind.

When a predator's chemical signature does show that it has recently fed on one of their own kind, prey fish take note!

Above: While adult guppies can swim in open water, new fry seek the protection of the weeds.

for hunters, not only because they are easy to swallow, but also because they are slower swimmers and quicker to tire if chased. For this reason, small fish are less likely to stray far from safety, remaining near to dense weed beds and seldom venturing out into open waters. Newborn livebearers often seek cover among floating plants, as there are fewer predators towards the top of the water column. Clumps of *Riccia* or similar vegetation act

as a refuge and can be a lifesaver in a community tank.

Q: *How do fish judge when it is safe to come out of hiding?*

A: In a risky situation fish may seek refuge but they have another imperative: they have to eat, as well as avoiding becoming food themselves. Sooner or later they have to come out. The unfortunate fact for small fish is that they have lower fat reserves than their larger brethren and cannot afford to shelter for as long. All in all, this means that the smallest fish have to be the boldest and the most adventurous, continuing to feed by necessity, even when threat levels send larger conspecifics into hiding.

Right: It can pay fish to keep close to a large predator. As well as monitoring its behavior, the presence of the large fish helps to frighten off smaller predators.

Hidden from danger

The aquatic environment is full of places to hide, if you know where to find them. Weed beds, rocky crevices, and even the substrate are all used by fish as hiding places. A good shelter is a valuable commodity and fish behave in a much more relaxed fashion if they know that such a refuge is nearby, often moderating their feeding patterns in order to stay close. In the wild, many fish species remain in one particular area for most of their adult lives. There are many reasons for this, but one of the most important is that staying in a familiar place is a safe option because if a predator shows up, the fish will know exactly what refuges are available and where to find them quickly.

Q: Do fish use the substrate as a refuge?

A: Hiding beneath the substrate is one type of refuge favored by eels and slender-bodied fish such as loaches. If danger threatens, a sudden dart can carry the fish into the bottom sand or mud and out of sight. Spiny eels and kuhli loaches actually spend a considerable amount of the day partially submerged, with only their heads showing. The added bonus is that as well as avoiding their predators, this strategy conceals them from the small animals that form their own diet and acts as an ideal place from which to mount an ambush.

Q: What happens if there is nowhere to hide?

A: Many fish improvise if they find themselves in a featureless environment, such as a bare aquarium. Some catfish seem to find reassurance by achieving contact with as many surfaces as possible, and may squeeze themselves into the corners or, if there are a few catfish, they may cluster together. This can happen even if a few basic shelters are provided. If they are too large, all the catfish may be found together under just one, again achieving the maximum amount of contact between their bodies and another surface, in this case other fish.

Below: A cluster of juvenile bagrid catfish gathered together in a crevice for safety. It would be hard for a predator to pick one out.

Right: The rocky shore habitats of Lake Malawi offer plenty of hiding places, all within easy reach of the more vulnerable fish.

Q: Do fish shelter in other underwater structures?

A: Just about any underwater formation can provide a gathering place for fish, be it natural structures such as aquatic plants, tree roots, and crevices in rocks, or even discarded litter, such as an old bicycle. The reason is that open water is a dangerous place to be. Being larger than their prey, predators can usually out swim them, but in a structured environment the smaller prey can outmaneuver their pursuers and squeeze themselves into gaps too small to admit the hunters. By assembling at such places, prey fish give themselves the best chance of avoiding danger – so long as they do not choose to gather at a predator's favorite hideout.

Left: Concealed within this clump of Ceratophyllum, *a young* Ctenochromis horei *shelters from danger.*

Q: Can fish hide in turbid water?

A: After rains and during stormy weather, even the clearest waters very often fill with fine, suspended mud and detritus, which drastically reduce visibility. For diurnal fish predators accustomed to hunting by sight in these clear waters, the inability to see their prey is a real handicap. It means that these turbid waters are a real boost to young fish, in particular, concealing them from predators and allowing them to feed uninterrupted.

Shaking off a tail

Refuges may prevent detection or prevent attack. Those that prevent detection by a predator are usually hiding places in one form or another. But prey animals sometimes head for areas where they know that predators may not be able to follow. As well as physical shelters, such as rocks, crevices, and weed beds, hunted fish often use their environment in remarkable ways.

Q: Are rapids good refuges for fish?

A: Whitewater rapids are an inhospitable place for fish, but those that adapt to live in such places gain the added benefit of escaping many of their predators. Several of the armored catfish come from exactly these conditions, where they are free to browse on algae and aufwuchs unmolested by other fish. Their powerful mouths are ideal, not only for feeding, but also for providing a great deal of purchase on the rocky substrate to prevent themselves from being washed away. Interestingly, female guppies are known to move into faster-flowing water to escape the constant persistence of males. The males cannot follow because their smaller body size limits their swimming ability and they would be simply swept away.

Q: Does migration work as a defense against predators?

A: Some species brave the physiological rigors of an estuarine environment where, again, many of their predators are unable to follow. And it is not only predators that find it hard going in the constantly shifting conditions at the sea's edge; parasites, including the dreaded freshwater variant of white spot, are swiftly killed by exposure to salt. But this ability has a downside – populations of mollies that have become adapted to brackish water are less resistant to white spot and can succumb to it if kept solely in fresh water.

Balancing risk and reward

Fish are often faced with trade-offs, none more so than guppies in the streams of Trinidad. Life in shallow water is safe, but there is little to eat.

Juveniles and males have to hide out in shallow water.

Larger females in deeper water cope with stronger currents and so face less food competition.

Predators are ready to snap up the unwary.

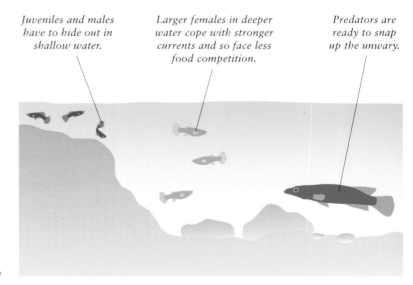

Left: *Walking catfish* (Clarias batrachus) *are famed for their ability to move across land in search of a new and safer home.*

Q: Can other tough environmental conditions be used by prey fish for shelter?

A: Moving to water that is low in dissolved oxygen may be one means by which prey fish can escape their predators. The swamp areas that fringe many larger lakes often act as a nursery for young fish, and the low oxygen levels found in many of these areas can sometimes prove too much for larger predators. In the mid-twentieth century, the introduction into Lake Victoria of the Nile perch brought about the extinction of hundreds of species of endemic cichlids similar to those found in the other Rift Lakes. But the story would have been far worse if the fish had not been able to seek refuge from the huge predator by moving out from the lake to the swampy margins and into a series of smaller satellite lakes, where the perch was unable to follow and where the fish were able to live unmolested.

Q: Do any fish take even more drastic measures to survive?

A: Extreme circumstances call for drastic action and on occasion, fish have been observed surviving against all odds, having managed to wait out some individual or collective disaster. In doing so, they have demonstrated themselves to be among the most adaptable animals on the planet – one reason for their success. The abilities of fish such as climbing perch and walking catfish have already been mentioned (see page 17), but perhaps the most footloose of fish is the mangrove killifish *(Kryptolebias marmoratus).* It makes its home in the smallest of water bodies, ranging from crab burrows to mere root holes in the mud and can move easily between each and every situation with flicks of its body. It can even withstand extended periods of emersion, surviving in damp leaf litter for days on end – one specimen survived happily for 66 days out of water.

Left: *The mangrove killifish* (Kryptolebias marmoratus) *is one of the most adaptable fish in the world, coping with extreme conditions and an hermaphroditic lifestyle.*

Behavioral defense

Even if the predator does detect its prey, the game is far from up. Fish have a variety of behavioral strategies available to them to avoid ending up as lunch. Beyond this, fish populations that co-exist with large numbers of predators often show adaptations that help them cope with this pressure. Some show additional behavioral defenses, others have developed different body shapes in response to predator cues, making them more difficult as targets. Others cope by maturing and producing offspring earlier.

Above: Glowlight tetras (Hemigrammus erythrozonus) are keenly sensitive to predator threats in their habitat.

Q: Can fish learn how to deal with predators?

A: If a fish can prevent its first encounter with a predator from being its last, it needs more than just the ability to learn quickly; it must be able to recognize the threat before it has even happened. But how on earth can this work? In fact, there are two ways. First of all, fish are born with the innate ability to recognize certain characteristics of predators, such as their body size and their large eyes and mouth. Secondly, they can learn from other members of their population. Many fish, including glowlight tetras (*Hemigrammus erythrozonus*), release a chemical alarm substance if they are injured. If another tetra comes across this smell, it reacts by taking evasive action. Fish are also able to link the smell of the alarm substance to the appearance of the predator in question, so that information about the danger passes through the population. In the case of the glowlight tetras, research has shown that the smell of the alarm substance causes the fish to show a much more dramatic response to the image of a cichlid than they might otherwise do. Once they have associated the cichlid with danger, the lesson remains learned.

Q: Can prey fish tell if a predator means business?

A: One way of learning about a predator is to take a closer look at it. Although this sounds potentially suicidal, it is precisely what prey fish of many different species do. As they approach they are careful to avoid what is known as the "attack cone" – the area immediately in front of the predator, where it might lunge forward to attack. By carrying out this predator inspection, fish can gather an incredible amount of information, including whether the predator has eaten recently and, if so, whether it has eaten

one of their own species (based on how it smells). From this they can gauge the level of the threat posed by the hunter. Often this inspection is carried out by only one or two individuals, the remainder of the local population remaining behind in safety. The risk to the inspectors is great but the pay-off for them can also be high. Studies have shown that males who carry out predator inspection become far more attractive to watching females.

Q: How do fish populations adjust to the presence of predators?

A: Many fish species show what is known as developmental plasticity. This simply means that as they develop they adapt to their conditions. Populations of fish that live alongside their predators develop deeper bodies compared to members of their own species from other

populations. This makes them harder for a predator to handle. As well as altered body shape, the hunted often show less vivid coloration. Male guppies from rivers that contain pike cichlids are far less bright than males that live apart from these piscivores. In addition to being less showy, the males from these populations also mature at an earlier age, giving them a better chance of breeding before they wind up as a meal.

The predator inspectors

One way to work out whether a predator means business is to get up close and inspect it.

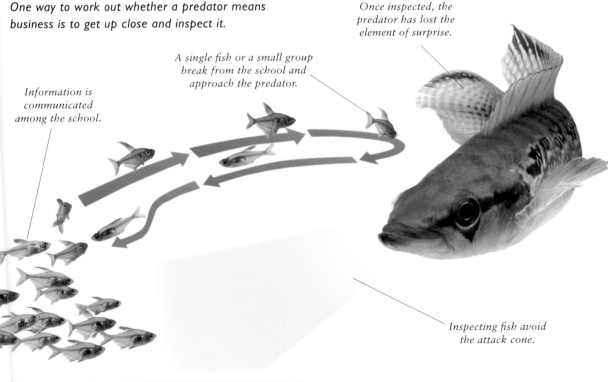

Once inspected, the predator has lost the element of surprise.

A single fish or a small group break from the school and approach the predator.

Information is communicated among the school.

Inspecting fish avoid the attack cone.

Chemical defenses

Several groups of animals produce poisons, either to use as venom to subdue their prey or for protection against their own predators, or even both. Poison arrow frogs are particularly notorious for their potent chemical defenses. But whereas a number of marine fishes use chemicals to deter overly inquisitive hunters, comparatively few freshwater fish have adopted this technique. However, those that do are worth treating with caution.

Above: Pufferfish are slow swimmers and use chemical defenses to discourage predators.

Left: If threatened, pufferfish can rapidly take in water and expand.

Q: How do pufferfish avoid predators?

A: Pufferfish have not one but two novel methods of overcoming predators, possibly as a result of their slow swimming speed, which might otherwise make them an easy target. The first line of defense is to swell up rapidly, taking huge volumes of water into their expandable stomachs. This sudden expansion usually leaves predators nonplussed, even unable to handle what has just become an unexpectedly large mouthful. But if this fails to produce the desired result, the back-up plan

is virtually foolproof. The internal organs of pufferfish, especially their livers and ovaries, contain a powerful neurotoxin called tetrodotoxin, which is 1,200 times more potent than cyanide. The amount produced varies by species; some produce sufficient to kill 30 humans.

Q: Do catfish spines contain venom?

A: As many fishkeepers know, a catfish removed from the

water will often lock out its leading pectoral and dorsal fin rays. This defensive reaction is in itself as damaging to predators in the wild as it is to a fish net at home, but some catfish species reinforce this physical defense with a chemical back-up. For instance, some fish in the *Pimelodella* genus have poison glands located at these spines which cause a reaction akin to a severe insect sting. However, perhaps the most dangerous of venomous catfish is the aptly named stinging catfish, *Heteropneustes fossilis*. A puncture wound from its pectoral spine can be fatal, even to humans. If you are unfortunate enough to be stung by a catfish, bathe the wound for as long as possible in the hottest water you can stand (which causes the venom to break down), while someone else calls the doctor.

Q: *Are stingrays dangerous?*

A: The name of the animal is the stingray, so perhaps it should come as no surprise that it packs a punch. That said, most stingray injuries are the result of unwary bathers stepping on the fish, which are usually concealed in the substrate – a situation that is clearly unlikely to occur in the home aquarium. The sting is a defensive mechanism, usually located towards the base of the tail, and jabbed upwards by the alarmed fish and into the leg of the victim. The fish are very seldom aggressive towards aquarium keepers; nonetheless, the increasing popularity of freshwater stingrays in the aquarium hobby increases the probability of an accidental injury and the animals should be handled with caution.

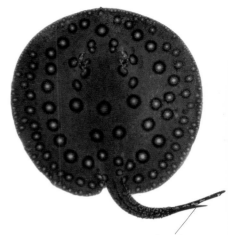

The sting is located at the end of the animal's tail.

Below: *Stingrays make fascinating aquarium subjects – so long as they are carefully handled!*

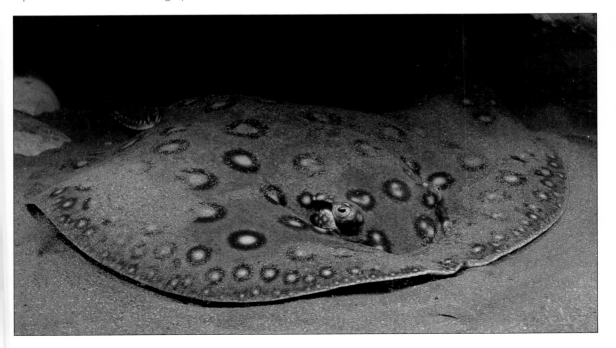

Fleeing from danger

Fish are extremely popular as prey among a diverse range of hunters. One reason is that they are an extremely rich source of food – fishes' bodies are packages of extremely lean swimming muscle that accounts for up to 80% of the fish's overall weight. But although this makes them an excellent menu item, it also means they can be tough to catch, so long as they become aware of the danger in good time.

Fish muscle groups

Fish are well supplied with muscle, enabling them not only to cruise around in the search for food but also to get out of a tight situation if needs be.

Red muscle is used by the body for sustained and steady activity.

White muscle provides power – but only for short periods.

Q: *What are the two main kinds of fish swimming muscles?*

A: In simple terms, there are two main kinds of muscle, distinguishable by their color. White muscle is used to provide explosive power of the kind used by human sprinters and weightlifters. White muscle is comparatively poorly supplied by the animal's circulating blood, hence its color. It provides a great deal of power, but only for a limited amount of time. This is because it operates anaerobically – without oxygen – and quickly becomes fatigued. Red muscle, by contrast, is very well supplied by the blood, as its color suggests, and is rich in oxygen. It provides steady, long-term power and is used by the animal as it cruises along.

Q: *Can fish swim out of danger?*

A: Quick reactions and a turn of speed are essential weapons for a fish when a predator makes an attack. Both of these are provided by white muscle and in most fish, this white muscle

accounts for a much higher proportion of the muscle mass than steady red muscle. This muscle bulk means that the fish can accelerate explosively from a slow or standing start – an essential defense against approaching danger.

Q: What's the best option for a fish that has been targeted by a predator?

A: Fish generally wait until the last moment to dart away. This

Below: A startled scissortail accelerates from a standing start with a burst of white muscle power – this turn of speed can be the difference between life and death.

is because the white muscle that powers this movement tires rapidly and if the fish sets off too soon it may merely alert the predator to its presence. By waiting until the threat is almost upon it, the fish can surprise its hunter and has a good chance of darting out of the predator's line of sight. Darting out of a home territory into uncharted waters can be dangerous – it could mean escaping from one predator only to blunder into another – so the sudden dash is something of a last resort. Many prey fish curl their body into a kind of "J" shape as danger approaches, ready to spring away with a powerful flick of the tail. Not only does this serve as preparation for a dash while the prey waits for the predator

to make the first move, it also signals to a stalking predator that it has been seen and that the game is up – "come any closer and I'm going."

▶ Netting fish

Netting a fish out of an aquarium can often try the patience, but by concentrating on one fish at a time, the aquarist can exploit the tendency of white muscle to fatigue quickly – few domestic fish can maintain escape speeds for over a minute.

By changing course and acting unpredictably while escaping, the fish can throw off its pursuer.

The chase is on

When a predator launches its attack, it is time for prey fish to get out of the way – and quickly. Of course, anywhere will do to start off with, so long as it is away from sharp teeth, but if a chase ensues, how should a fish behave? Swimming along a predictable path could allow the predator to second guess its intention, but if it swims randomly, an individual could become isolated from its school, making it an easy target.

Q: *Where should fish head for if attacked?*

A: Once a fish has decided to take evasive action, its next move will determine whether it lives or dies. For fish that live in the first few feet above the river or lake bed, the first move is almost always downwards, angling sharply towards the safety offered by rocks or plants. On the other hand, those that live at the top of the water column steer towards the surface, possibly taking advantage of any background of overhanging branches, etc., to break up their outline and make it difficult for the hunter to spot them.

Q: *I've sometimes noticed my fish swimming unusually when scared. What's happening?*

A: Fish under attack often adopt a swimming behaviour known as "skittering." This refers to the way they dart about rapidly in an apparently haphazard fashion, turning sharply in different directions and making it hard for predators to catch them. As a general rule, predators are larger than their prey and, therefore, faster swimmers, so it would make little sense for an escaping prey fish to dash in a straight line – the predator would simply overtake and capture it. However, the size of the predator also makes it less maneuverable and it is this factor that the prey exploit with the sharp banks and turns seen during skittering. Even so, fish can only play this game for a short time – skittering quickly exhausts them – so to be safe, they must quickly find a hiding place.

Evading by hiding

Being larger, predators are excluded from small refuges.

The loach can find safety among a tangle of roots and stones.

Sometimes skittering succeeds in shaking off a predator, but with a really persistent predator, the prey fish double back and fall in behind the predator, accepting this rather dubious and possibly shortlived haven.

Q: Can any fish fly out of trouble?

A: Freshwater hatchetfish get their name from their extremely deep chests, which in conjunction with their slender caudal peduncle, makes them resemble a hatchet, or axe. This enlarged chest region holds the

Evading by flying

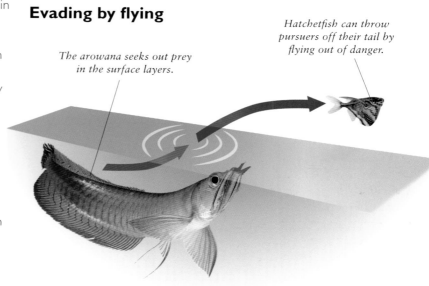

The arowana seeks out prey in the surface layers.

Hatchetfish can throw pursuers off their tail by flying out of danger.

Evading by skittering

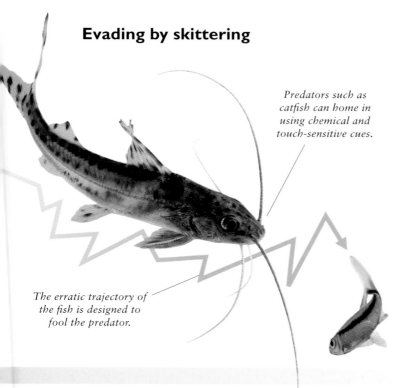

Predators such as catfish can home in using chemical and touch-sensitive cues.

The erratic trajectory of the fish is designed to fool the predator.

massive muscles that power their sizeable pectoral fins. Why does the fish need such dramatic fins and musculature? The answer is equally dramatic: it is the only type of fish that is capable of true powered flight. Unlike the flying fishes of the ocean, which simply jump and glide, hatchetfish are able to beat their winglike pectoral fins and propel themselves in a straight line for a few feet before returning to the water. They use this remarkable ability not only to catch flying insects but also to evade predators. One quick leap and they are able to distance themselves from their no doubt astonished hunter.

A tough mouthful

Of course, not every fish darts away as a predator approaches. Some fish have evolved armor and other defenses, most often in the shape of spines, to make all but the meanest of predators seek their dinner elsewhere. But if it is so effective, why have not all fish evolved armor plating? The reason is that armor is heavy and cumbersome. For fish that live on the bottom, such as many catfish, this is not a problem, but for fish that need to hunt elusive prey such as insect larvae and copepods in the water column, the handicap of armor would be too great.

Q: What is fish armor made of?

A: The armored plates, more correctly known as "scutes," found on many catfish are not scales. In fact, no catfishes have true scales as other fish do. Instead, the scutes are made up from the epidermis, or skin, of the animal and overlap to provide a tough barrier

against predators. The strength of these scutes is provided by their constituent structural proteins, just as in animals such as lobsters and beetles. Providing there are enough minerals in the water to aid the growth of the scutes, the armor develops early in life. However, the smallest fish need speed to evade predators and so do not develop the full extent of the armor until later in life.

Q: Who needs armor and where and when?

A: The physiological investment involved in making armor is considerable. As a result, differences exist between populations according to

Below: The wide, locking pectoral spines of this anchor catfish (Hara jerdoni) *make it a tough proposition for any predator.*

whether they live alongside predators or not. Populations that live alongside their hunters often develop thicker body armor than those that do not. This is partly controlled by the genes of the fish and partly develops in response to the presence of predator cues in the water during their early life. Another factor is which parts of the body to protect; again this is a trade-off between security and the weight of the armor. Consequently, most armored fish have their thickest defenses around their heads and across their backs. The undersides of many armored catfish, which are usually pressed against the substrate, are often quite soft.

Q: How else can a fish's body structure help it to overcome predators?

A: Spines are an excellent way of protecting oneself against predators. They fulfill two main purposes. Firstly, they can physically damage an aggressor; sharp tips and serrated edges are perfectly capable of wounding a foe, be it a rival or a predator. Secondly, you may have noticed how many species of fish lock out their fin rays when they are disturbed, especially the leading rays of their pectoral and dorsal fins. This has the effect of increasing the girth of the fish — making it wider than the mouth of a piscivorous fish or a bird's throat and thus almost impossible to swallow. The spines can be locked into place using a specialized socket and offer an extremely stubborn defense. The effectiveness of the spines in saving the lives of catfishes was demonstrated by a study that reported that out of ten attacks made on catfish, where the predator actually managed to

get the prey into its mouth, the presence of the spines meant that in all but one instance, the catfish were ejected unharmed from the predator's mouth.

Left: A serrated row of scutes along the flank of this talking catfish (Platydoras costatus) could easily damage soft throat tissue.

Acanthicus adonis *gains protection with a spiny skin and toughened dorsal and pectoral fin rays.*

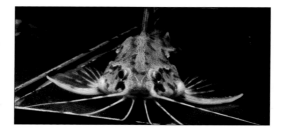

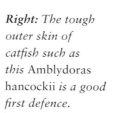

Right: The tough outer skin of catfish such as this Amblydoras hancockii *is a good first defence.*

The enemy within

Although we have been mainly concerned with the kinds of predators that might eat a fish, it is an unfortunate fact of life for wild fishes that this tells only half the story. Parasites are everywhere in the wild, and it is a rare fish that does not harbor some parasites, perhaps even thousands, during the course of its life.

Q: What exactly is a parasite?

A: A parasite is a general term for any animal that gains all or part of its nutrition from another, usually larger, animal. Some parasites, such as fish lice, live outside their hosts, making a connection only when they want to feed. Others live inside, eating their host from the inside out.

Q: How can fish avoid parasites?

A: In simple terms, they cannot avoid them completely, but they do have an inbuilt resistance, more effective in some individuals than in others. For example, a healthy, well-fed adult will be less prone than a juvenile or weak fish. In addition, fish have

A natural salt bath

Fish such as mollies that can cope with variable salinity, can use this ability to rid themselves of parasites.

Moving into the saltwater of the estuary stresses or kills many freshwater parasites.

The parasites die and are shed, allowing wounds to heal.

Parasites are a perennial problem for wild fish.

some behavioral tricks to help them avoid parasites. Some fish are known to move between freshwater and the estuaries of their river, thereby applying a salt bath to control the parasites. Most shoo ling fish are able to recognize when a conspecific is parasitized and avoid it if possible.

Q: How do parasites get onto or inside a fish in the first place?

A: The ways of parasites are many and devious. Some, such as bacteria and fungus that cause infections, and others, such as the protozoans responsible for white spot disease, are present in the water all the time and are able to attack when a fish is weakened, stressed, or wounded. Others use some surprising tactics. Fish lice actively hunt their victims using smell and vision and are especially attracted to anything shiny which, underwater, usually means a fish. Fluke worms, such as *Gyrodactylus*, cause the fish that they infect to clamp their fins and wave their bodies, a behavior sometimes known as "shimmying." This behavior apparently causes other fish to approach and investigate, putting them at greater risk of infection, as well as creating a

Left: Fish lice can cause a significant drain on a fish's resources.

A parasite life cycle

Parasites with more than one host have some ingenious ways of moving between their different host species.

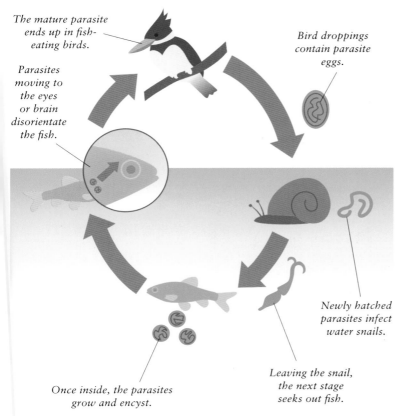

The mature parasite ends up in fish-eating birds.

Parasites moving to the eyes or brain disorientate the fish.

Bird droppings contain parasite eggs.

Newly hatched parasites infect water snails.

Leaving the snail, the next stage seeks out fish.

Once inside, the parasites grow and encyst.

small local current of water that the parasites can use to disperse, almost like a sneeze can carry cold germs between humans. The larvae of trematode worms infect the tiny invertebrates that fish feed on, such as *Cyclops* and *Daphnia*. When a fish eats one, the parasite enters its unwitting host like the Trojan horse.

Q: Do parasites change fishes' behavior?

A: Some parasites have complex life cycles that require them to move between different hosts as they mature. In many cases, the parasites move from the fish into predatory birds. For this to occur, the bird must eat an infected fish. To maximize the chances of this happening, parasites can alter the behavior of the fish, so that it is more likely to be eaten. One parasite that infects killifish damages the fish's brain and makes it swim erratically at the surface of the water. Others lodge in the lens of their host fish's eye, preventing the victim from seeing an approaching predator. The tapeworm *Ligula* seems capable of making its fish host completely fearless, so that instead of dashing for cover when danger threatens, it hangs around, often with fatal consequences.

Chapter 6
Schooling

A huge number of different fish school. It is estimated that over half of the 25,000 or so known fish species school at some point during their lives. The incredibly widespread use of this strategy among fish species is an indication of its value.

Schooling provides individual fish with significant benefits. It reduces each individual fish's risk of predation, helping it to find food more easily and to save energy through the hydrodynamic advantages of swimming in a group.

Q: Is there a difference between a shoal and a school?

A: Both words refer to a group of fish. Some people try to make a distinction between them, saying that in a school the individuals tend to be more closely knit as a unit, more polarized—all facing or swimming the same way—as opposed to shoaling, where the group is much less cohesive. Fish, however, do not respect this distinction, and often the division is quite blurry. In fact, the appropriate term can change from moment to moment. Thus, it has no useful biological reality, and it is unimportant for aquarists. Throughout this book we use the term "school" to indicate a group of fish of any type.

Q: Who schools and who doesn't in the fish world?

A: Different fish use the schooling strategy to different extents. A few species, such as herring, are known as "obligate" schoolers, meaning they are compelled to live in the social group and will rapidly die if isolated. Most species are "facultative" schoolers, using the advantages of schooling when it suits them and disbanding at other times, say, when food arrives. Many species use schooling at some stage in their life cycle, usually when they are small and vulnerable to predators, before abandoning the strategy as they grow larger and older. Cichlids are a good example. As juveniles they live in groups, but when they mature they leave the safety of the school to establish themselves in their own territories. Most familiar aquarium fish species school in early life. Bitterling (temperate fish) lay their eggs

Right: A school of harlequin rasboras (Trigonostigma heteromorpha). Living in a group like this offers protection for such small and vulnerable fish.

inside freshwater mussels and the larvae school as soon as they emerge from the mantle cavity of the mollusc.

Q: *When should fish school?*

A: Schooling works extremely well as an anti-predator strategy, but it also has costs. Living in a group means fighting many competitors to gain a share of any resource. Fish tend more to form schools when they feel threatened, for example, when a predator is around, when they move into a new and unfamiliar environment or when they are in open water with no nearby hiding places to dash into. Schooling only works against

Above: *Silver tetras* (Hasemania *spp.*) *in a tight-knit School. Fish sometimes pack together like this in response to a threat.*

visual predators – those that hunt using sight. At night, fish schools often tend to break up because concentrated schools of fish actually attract hunters that use smell to locate their prey.

How schooling works

Schools of fish can consist of just two or three fish or over a million. Some species form huge schools, such as the grey mullet in the Caspian Sea, whose schools may extend for an incredible 60 miles (100 km). But irrespective of the species in question or the size of school it forms, the basic principles about schools are the same. What looks to be an extremely complicated and choreographed behavior is in fact beautifully simple and this simplicity underlies its success.

Q: *How do fish form schools?*

A: Individual fish gravitate together and are held there by the forces of social attraction. Among fish such as tetras, this attraction exerts an extremely powerful pull; individuals are strongly drawn to conspecifics and even to individuals of other closely related species. If a school of fish is attacked and the members of the school scatter, individuals may find themselves isolated. Solitary fish become highly stressed as a result of their segregation and urgently try to locate others by sight or using longer-range chemical cues. If and when they detect these cues, they rapidly home in on their source and rejoin those fish until eventually the entire school reforms. Similarly, schools break up as darkness falls each evening, but reform at dawn every day as individual fish seek out and stick together with conspecifics.

Fish personal spaces

The structure of the school is maintained by simple forces – each fish has a "zone of attraction" and a "zone of repulsion."

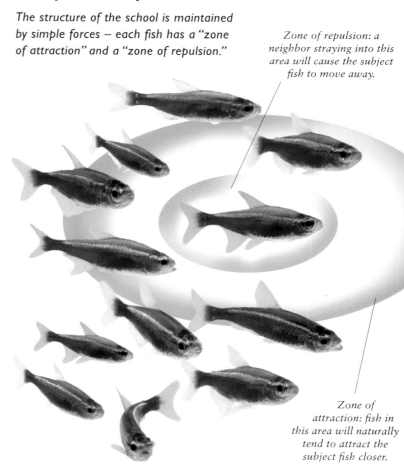

Zone of repulsion: a neighbor straying into this area will cause the subject fish to move away.

Zone of attraction: fish in this area will naturally tend to attract the subject fish closer.

Q: How close do fish within a school get to one another?

A: From the tiniest tetras to the huge ocean-going tunas, schools of fish almost always maintain a steady distance between themselves and their nearest neighbors. This distance relates to the length of the fish. Under normal circumstances, fish in schools tend to keep between two and three body lengths apart. Thus, a school of 1-inch (2-cm) long fish will keep a distance of 1.5 to 2 inches (4 to 5 cm) between themselves and their nearest neighbors. These distances are governed by the situation that the fish find themselves in. Nearest neighbor distances increase when fish are hungry and scouring their habitat for food, and decrease when fish are threatened or swimming against a fast current, causing the school to coalesce.

Q: How do fish keep their schools together?

A: Fish use all their sensory abilities to keep tabs on their schoolmates. The sense of smell is important for recognizing school members and locating the school if it moves out of sight. The sensation of touch, via the lateral line, is essential if fish are to polarize and move coherently with the rest of the school.

However, the most important sensory input comes from the eyes. Although blind fish are capable of schooling, fish primarily use vision to maintain contact with the school. Many schooling species, including X-ray tetras (*Pristella maxillaris*), signal to each other using bold bars, often sited on their dorsal or caudal fins or along their bodies. In the case of X-ray tetras, the fish flick their banded dorsal fin to help keep the school together and show an increase in their rate of fin-flicking when they feel threatened. Research on this also found that X-ray tetras without the bars on their fins were much less socially attractive to conspecifics, causing schools to be less coherent.

Right: In common with all schooling fish, X-ray tetras (Pristella maxillaris) *show strong social attraction to one another and maintain their Schools with visual signals.*

Synchronized swimming

One of the most arresting sights in the whole animal kingdom is that of a school of fish turning this way and that in perfect harmony with their schoolmates. It seems almost impossible to believe that an animal supposedly as simple as a fish could execute such a well-choreographed routine so beautifully, and yet they do. Of course, this impression is slightly exaggerated. When it comes down to the nuts and bolts of schooling behavior, the fish are not choreographed at all, but simply responding to localized cues. Nonetheless, the effect it produces is beautiful but much easier to understand.

Q: So how exactly do fish in schools stay in such perfect synchrony with each other?

A: No matter how large the school, each fish in it has a relatively small number of near neighbors. The behavior of these nearby fishes exerts a strong influence on each individual fish to the extent that it simply copies what they do. When a school turns, say, when it meets an underwater obstacle or encounters a danger, the movement almost always begins with a single fish or at most a small number of fish. Those

nearest the turning fish will, in the absence of any other information, replicate that movement. Then those next to them also turn and in this fashion the signal transmits across the whole school. Slowed right down using video footage, you can see a wave of activity passing through the school. This phenomenon is sometimes known as the "Trafalgar effect," presumably because of the way that the firing of the cannons on the flagship brought about the firing of guns in the rest of the fleet like a domino topple. The most amazing thing about a school turning like this is the speed with which the signal to turn is

School shapes

The overall shape of a fish school changes according to what the fish are doing. When the fish are searching for food, for example, the school spreads out to form a wide front like a search party. In contrast, when the school is under threat, the fish tend to move in together to form a ball.

Schools changing direction

A change in direction by one group member can spread throughout that group and be copied by group members in fractions of a second.

1 *An external influence, perhaps a predator or the smell of food, is detected by the leader.*

2 *The leader's response is to turn and take a new course, cutting across those swimming behind.*

Right: Schools of fish in the wild, such as this group of Enantiopus melanogenys *in Lake Tanganyika, can include hundreds or even thousands of tightly packed individuals.*

conveyed throughout the school. This rapid response is brought about in part by the need of each individual fish not to stand out from the crowd. Those that do may be picked out by a predator (see page 122).

Q: Does the school act more like a single, large animal than just a collection of individuals?

In many respects, yes. Although each fish has its own identity, the school sometimes seems to operate as if it has a life of its own. This is particularly apparent when a school "senses" its environment. Schools of fish are excellent at sensing the various stimuli in their surroundings, far better than a similar-sized, simple, loose collection of individual fish. If different members of the school detect the odor of food and each turns towards it, not all will be exactly accurate in their course, but the average direction that all the detecting fish set a course for – the direction that eventually the school will head in – is usually extremely precise. This effect is sometimes referred to as the "wisdom of crowds" and is also seen in humans. For example, if 100 people at a fairground stall are asked to guess the number of sweets in a jar, their individual guesses may be wide of the mark but the average of their guesses is often remarkably accurate.

3 *This turning motion is usually then copied by the fish nearest to the leader.*

4 *These fish are in turn copied until the whole group assumes a new traveling direction.*

Safety in numbers

The single most important benefit that fish gain from schooling is thought to be the reduction of predation risk. Schooling works in a number of ways to confound hunters, but the net effect – survival of the school members – has been shown again and again.

Q: *Can a predator sneak up on a school?*

A: To hunt successfully, most predators need the element of surprise. They must approach sufficiently close to their quarry so that when they attack, their victim has no opportunity to flee. But as we have seen, the sensory abilities of all the individuals in a school combine to provide excellent long-range detection. As a result, the school is likely to be aware of the approaching danger, because of its "many eyes," even before the predator itself has detected the school. With the advantage of this early warning, the fish in the school draw close together and behave in a much more uniform fashion.

Q: *What is meant by the "confusion effect"?*

A: Although some predators attack blindly, rushing at the school in the hope of snagging a fish at random, this approach rarely works effectively. Instead, hunters usually try to select a victim before attacking, picking out an individual and chasing it down. This causes grouping fish to select their schoolmates with care, strongly preferring to associate with conspecifics of the same size and color to produce schools of near identical fish. Faced with such a mass of like-for-like fish, the predator is overloaded with choice and becomes "confused." This often has the effect of delaying an attack or causing the predator to abandon it altogether. However, if one school member has chosen its schoolmates poorly and is somehow different from the other school members, say, larger than them, the predator can often overcome the confusion effect and catch out the odd one. Therefore, schooling fish that are in any way different are at huge risk of being picked out, which is why they are all so similar in terms of their color patterns, body shape, and even behavior.

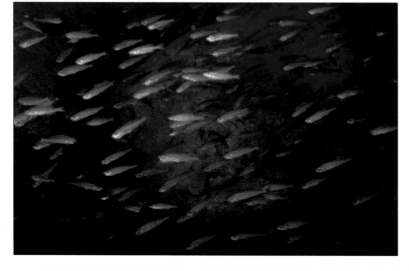

Left: The overwhelming number of apparently identical fish in this school of Cyprichromis leptosoma *makes it hard for a predator to target one individual.*

Q: How else might fish in a school survive against predators?

A: One important benefit of being in a school is known as "attack dilution." Most predators are only capable of capturing one victim at a time. Therefore, even if a predator makes a successful attack, a fish in a school of 100 others has only a 1% chance of being unlucky. In this way, the risk of being the chosen one is diluted among the members of the school. It means that in high-risk situations it pays to be in the largest school possible. Convict cichlid parents exploit these mathematical probabilities in a remarkably clever way. In the wild they "kidnap" the fry of other pairs and add them to their own brood, thus diluting the risk to their own offspring. To make this even more effective, studies have shown that they preferentially kidnap fry that are slightly smaller than their own and therefore less skilled at evading attack. If a predator does attack the brood, the foster fry suffer a disproportionately greater amount of risk, leaving the pair's own young safer than might otherwise be the case and without adding any substantial extra guarding costs to the parental fish.

Above: Although the parent fish watches diligently, young fry must depend on the protection of the school if they are not to succumb to predators at an early age.

Below: An attack causes some of the fish towards the bottom left to become partially separated from the group. Within seconds they start to close ranks once more.

Finding and fighting for food

Although schools work mostly to defeat predators, the combined senses of many individuals in the group also prove to be excellent at locating food patches in their environment. The result is that fish in schools find food a great deal faster than if they were hunting alone. And there are other benefits to schooling. For example, fish in traveling schools also save considerable amounts of energy by swimming in the slipstream of leading fish. But set against all these advantages, there is one major cost: competition. Fish in schools live among their greatest competitors. Although schools are good at locating food, there is rarely enough to go around for all the school members, and this means that all but the most dominant are left hungry. This can be a significant cost and, as a result, fish must weigh the pros and cons of schooling according to the situation.

Q: How do fish decide when to school and when to go it alone?

A: In each situation they experience, schooling fish are fairly well able to assess the risks. If danger is lurking, fish very seldom actively choose to leave the safety of the school. If a situation does not appear to be especially risky, and if they are hungry, fish may venture away from the group to try to find some food for themselves. A great deal of research has been done on the habitats occupied by guppies in their home streams of Trinidad in the Caribbean. Some of these streams are also home to pike cichlids and blue acaras, which like nothing more than to feast on the small livebearers. In such streams the guppies form extremely tight, cohesive schools as a defensive measure. Other populations of guppies that live free from the depredations of the cichlids have all but abandoned schooling behavior.

Left: Guppies in their natural river habitats in Trinidad face a wide range of predators, including pike cichlids and acaras.

Q: How can fish get an advantage over their schoolmates in the scramble for food?

A: To find food, schooling fish can either seek it out for themselves or keep a very close eye on the other fish in the school. If they detect that another fish has found a food patch, they will often home in and stake their claim to a share. This kind of exploitation of others is sometimes referred to as "informational parasitism." And it is not just members of the school that look out for feeding fish; predators keep close tabs on them as well and often concentrate their attacks on the feeders who may be far less vigilant because they are distracted by their feeding.

Above: Zebra danios (Danio rerio) *gather into a tight bunch during a feeding frenzy. Injuries can easily occur at this time.*

Picking the right moment

When selecting a potential victim, predators can shift the odds in their own favor by attacking prey animals that aren't paying attention.

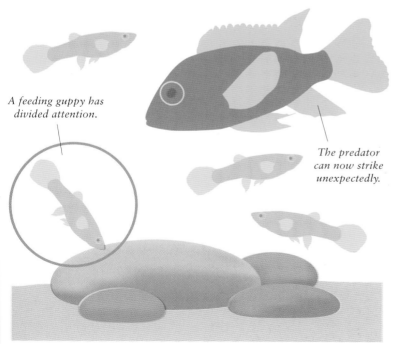

A feeding guppy has divided attention.

The predator can now strike unexpectedly.

Q: Do schooling fish ever become aggressive with each other?

A: Schooling would be a poor strategy if the fish in a group spent all their time fighting. As a result, schooling fish are usually extremely peaceable. But this apparent harmony can occasionally vanish. If a school comes across a rich and concentrated food source, it is a case of every fish for itself. Zebra danios are among the least aggressive of all community fish, but studies have shown that their peaceful nature can be easily disrupted when there is a scramble for food. Slow-motion film shows that they nip, block, and charge one another as they try to obtain the greatest possible share for themselves.

125

Picking a place

Schooling fish must balance the safety provided by the group against the cost of sharing their food. But this does not necessarily mean that they have to leave the school if they want to eat well, or that their only chance of avoiding being eaten is to stick like glue to their schoolmates. The real world is not as simple as that. Instead, fish can move to different positions in the school because the benefits and costs change according to whether they are at the front or the back, the middle or the edge.

at the fringes of the school that find the best food and face the greatest amount of danger.

Q: Are some school positions better than others?

A: The risks and rewards that each fish gets from schooling depend on its place in the school. Fish at the front of a moving school get the first pick of the food and can take the tastiest morsels for themselves, while those further back have to be content with the scraps. But to balance this, the fish at the front of a school are also the first to bump into predators, so they face the greatest risks. In stationary schools, it is the fish

Q: Do fish change their position in the school?

A: Schooling fish are actually very good at balancing risk against reward. When a fish is hungry it usually responds by slightly increasing its swimming speed, picking up the pace to try to find food. This increase in speed means that they gradually move to the front of the school, where they can get more food at the expense of greater risk. Once they have satisfied their hunger, they gradually move back towards the middle of the school where they are safer from attack.

Above: Cichlid parents abandon their young in the nests of Bagrus meridionalis. *The young cichlids bear the brunt of predator attacks.*

Consequently, fish in schools tend to circulate between positions at the front of the group and in the middle according to how hungry they are.

Q: Do fish in a school co-operate with one another, or are they selfish?

A: When a school of fish is threatened, the fish on the outside try to get into the comparative safety of the middle. However, those already in the middle have no desire to be

pushed to the outside, so they hold their ground. The net effect is that the school becomes highly compact. These attempts to hide behind other members of the group and to get to safety at their expense was termed "selfish herd" behavior by the famous biologist Bill Hamilton. But schooling fish are not always selfish; there is strong evidence to suggest that in some circumstances, say, when they choose feeding partners or fish to accompany them on predator inspection missions, they choose individuals or relatives they already know to be co-operative.

Q: How else do fish exploit the position benefits of schooling?

A: In Lake Malawi, some cichlids are known to leave their young in the nests of parental bagrid catfish. But the catfish do not simply accept their status as victims in all this. When the eggs hatch, they force the young cichlids to the edge of the school of fry and keep their own young in the center. The pay-off for the catfish is that when predators attack the nest, they are seven times more likely to capture a young cichlid than one of their own offspring. Thus, the cichlid fry act as an effective buffer between the catfish fry and the predator.

Fish leaders and followers

The position that a fish occupies in a school can determine both the amount of food it obtains, as well as the risk it faces from predators.

Leading fish reach food first.

Fish in the middle face fewer risks.

1 *Hungry fish tend to swim more quickly than sated fish, causing them to move forward.*

2 *A slower swimming speed after feeding means the fish drops back into the group.*

Who's who in the fish school

For fish that live in schools, just as in human society, it pays to choose your associates carefully. In fact, it could be said to be even more important to fish than to people, because the wrong choice for a fish could put it at risk of being eaten.

Q: *What sort of things do they look at when deciding on a schoolmate?*

A: When fish decide whether to join a school, they assess a host of different factors. Given a choice,

they prefer to school with fish of the same species as themselves. After this, they favor fish that are the same size and color. And it does not end there; fish that have parasites or are behaving in an unusual way are shunned. All the different criteria that fish use to select their schoolmates mean that schools of fish in the wild are often composed of remarkably similar individuals, presenting a united front of uniformity to predators.

Q: *Why must fish choose?*

A: Fish schools only work effectively when all the school

members are closely matched in terms of their appearance and behavior. By choosing individuals just like themselves as schoolmates, fish can be fairly sure that these individuals are more likely to behave in the same way, to have similar swimming abilities, to live in the same kinds of habitats and to prefer to eat the same kinds of foods – all in all, a kind of fishy comfort zone. If one individual stands out from the crowd, it is much easier for a predator to select this fish as a victim. The interesting thing is that "odd" fish seem to be only too aware of how conspicuous they are and, understandably, behave extremely nervously. Studies have shown that although the largest fish in a school could theoretically bully the other fish if they had to compete for food, they often eat very little compared to the others, especially if they sense danger.

Q: *How good are they at choosing?*

A: Given the cost of making the wrong decision, it is perhaps not surprising that schooling fish are excellent at discriminating

Tetra schoolmates

1 *Schools of fish in the wild are not closed shops – members join or leave frequently.*

2 *Within larger schools, subgroups of up to ten fish may stick together for longer periods.*

3 *Subgroups, as in the tetras here, are usually made up of very closely matched fish.*

between potential schoolmates if they have a choice of schools to join. Fish show strong preferences to associate with individuals that are the same size as themselves. They are excellent at this matching behavior and usually actively choose fish that are within about 10% of their own size. An interesting, and as yet unanswered, question is how do fish know how large they are – there are no mirrors underwater! But the fact remains that they can and do discriminate. However, fish do not always have a choice of schools to join, and the cost to a schooling fish of being isolated far outweighs that of being in a less-than-perfect school. Species of fish that rely on schooling for safety often have a very short life expectancy if they strike out on their own for any length of time. It is far better for them to join an unusual school and then to make a switch if and when the opportunity arises. For this reason, schools in the wild are sometimes made up of a hotch-potch of different fish, but if a predator comes into view, they tend miraculously to separate into subgroups of matching fish.

Life in the group

A considerable number of tropical aquarium fish spend their entire lives within a school, but the extent to which they congregate depends on their perception of danger, or the need to feed or breed.

1 *This group of red phantom tetras is slightly dispersed as school members forage for food particles in the water column.*

2 *Suddenly, the group is disturbed by some potential threat. A moment later the fish are packed together and polarized.*

Chapter 7
War and peace

To the casual observer, a tropical aquarium can seem one of the most serene environments, but this apparent calm is often an illusion; nature is frequently just as red in tooth and claw within the aquarium as it is beyond its glass walls.

Part of the skill of fishkeeping is to select compatible individuals and species, but fish will still regularly squabble among themselves, even within the confines of the aquarium. In order to create an environment where fish can prosper, it is important to understand what they might fight over and why. But against this background of continual strife, various studies carried out in recent years have shown that fish may also co-operate with each other in the day-to-day struggle for survival. These compelling examples have shown that fish are master strategists, fighting when they have to and combining forces at other times.

Q: *What sorts of things do fish fight over?*

A: Fish almost always fight over the same thing – scarce resources.

Be it food, space, or mates, fish fight when there is not enough to go around, and the winner's reward is the lion's share of the available supplies. How hard they fight depends on what is at stake: if the squabble is only over a meal, the battle will be far less fierce than when two fish are struggling for the attentions of the only female.

Q: *How do fish settle their disputes?*

A: Actual fighting is very rare among fish. Although they may bicker and peck at one another fairly frequently, full-scale fights do not happen every day. When a dispute arises between fishes, the protagonists usually engage in protracted displays towards one another. These displays convey to an opponent everything it needs to know about how tough its task will be if it continues to be aggressive. Most disputes are settled during this stage. It is only

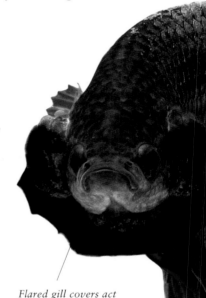

Flared gill covers act as a threat gesture.

when two opponents are very closely matched that these preliminary displays fail to settle a score and real fights break out.

Q: *Do all fish fight?*

A: Most species of fish fight when they have to, though some seem

*Flowing fins
demonstrate prowess.*

> ### Fighting fish
>
> The Siamese fighting fish
> (*Betta splendens*) gained
> notoriety for its combative
> lifestyle. Males fight to the
> death if kept together. In the
> aquarium, house a pair or
> one male to two females, but
> never more than one male.

Q: When and why do fish choose to co-operate?

A: There are many instances where two or more fish can accomplish things that a solitary fish cannot, from raising offspring to getting rid of parasites. When this is the case, it would be a foolish fish that does not co-operate. The remarkable thing about all the examples of co-operation between fish is that, in many cases, it requires a level of intelligence that many people did not credit them with. Over recent years, more and more evidence has accumulated on fish co-operation. It is clear now that co-operation is not so unusual in fishes' day-to-day activities, but is a vital part of their behavioral repertoire.

to fight more than others. Species that take territories, such as cichlids, or that form dominance hierarchies, such as platies and swordtails, are more aggressive than those that do not, but once territories are marked out and dominance hierarchies are decided, even these fish do not fight much.

Food fights

If you were to reduce a fish's behavior right down to the basics, you would see that just about everything stems from three main imperatives: the need to avoid predators, the need to feed on a day-to-day basis, and the need to breed successfully over the course of their lives. Fish have a wide range of ingenious strategies for avoiding predators and for breeding, but the need to gather energy to support the rest of their behavior is no less challenging. Fish of different species feed on just about every kind of available organic matter, from a huge variety of animals and plants to the detritus that gathers at the bottom of the water column. Apart from the possible exception of a few highly specialized feeders, all face competition for their food from members of their own species as well as others. Those that gain the largest share of food for themselves are also the most likely to be successful at avoiding predators and, ultimately, breeding. With such a lot at stake it is perhaps not surprising that the foragers are prepared to fight for their share.

Q: When are feeding fish at their most aggressive?

A: There are three main conditions under which fish are most likely to fight for food, and all have to do with economics. If fish can get more food by fighting for it, there is a pretty good chance they will. The first reason that fish might squabble relates to the amount of food available to them. Studies on White Cloud Mountain minnows have shown that if there is very little food, fish often prefer to save their energy rather than waste it in fighting. Similarly, fish rarely fight when there is plenty of food to

Fair shares for all

The way food is distributed in the environment has a huge effect on how the fish themselves are spread out and how aggressive they may become towards one another.

When food is spread evenly through the habitat, so too are the fish. This usually leads to harmony.

If much food is concentrated in one small area, some individuals may try aggressively to exclude others.

There is no point defending a rich food patch if there are many other fish around – you cannot fight everyone.

go around; to do so would be a waste of energy. But when there is just about enough for all, the strongest fish often try to take not only their own share but also that of their weaker schoolmates. Secondly, fish aggression increases when food is concentrated into one particular space. If it is spread fairly evenly around their habitat, it is hard for the dominant fish to prevent the others from getting their portion. Finally, research on blue gouramis (*Trichogaster trichopterus*) has shown that the fish tend to be more aggressive when the number of rivals to fight off is relatively small; a bully can fight off a few competitors, but

can become swamped by larger numbers and therefore fights less.

Q: Who is most likely to win a fight over food?

A: Size counts for a great deal in all types of fish fights; large fish are usually dominant. But equally, the likelihood of a dominant fish beating the competition to grab some food depends on the type of competition. "Scramble" competition, where the first on the scene gets the food, favors fast fish and aggression does not usually come into it. Alternatively, "contest" competition, where fish fight it out to get to a food

Above: Serpae tetras around a food tablet in a race to see who can eat the most in the shortest time.

resource, definitely does benefit stronger, more aggressive fish. Sometimes, a dominant fish will even steal the food right out of the mouth of one of its rivals. If the forager cannot fit all its food into its mouth, it may be harassed by others and even have its meal torn from it by a stronger competitor. For this reason, subordinate fish in competitive situations tend to be highly selective over their portion sizes.

Feeding territories

While all fish will fight to try to make sure they get as much food as possible, some species take this a step further and stake a claim for a feeding territory, excluding all their rivals from a patch of their habitat and keeping all the food supplies for themselves.

Q: *Which fish defend feeding territories?*

A: For a fish to go to the extent of defending a feeding territory – a behavior that uses up considerable time and energy – there has to be considerable benefit. The territory must provide the fish with plenty of food and that food usually has to be renewable. African Rift Lake cichlids are a good example of this, defending what are sometimes referred to as algal gardens. The algae grow slowly but continuously, providing a steady harvest for any fish prepared

to defend it. Territories can also provide other benefits. Fish such as red-tailed black sharks and some loach species, for example the skunk loach, often defend a patch of their environment aggressively, keeping for themselves not only the food that the territory provides, but also certain favored sheltering spots within it.

Q: *What happens to the fish that cannot get a territory?*

A: This behavior of territory holders can sometimes force subordinates to change their behavioral strategy completely. This might include switching to being active at a different time of day or moving into less productive parts of a habitat, away from the attentions of the territory holders.

Left: In the aquarium, red-tailed black sharks (Epalzeorhynchos bicolor) *are often intolerant of other members of their own species.*

Below: Loaches, like this Yasuhikotakia sidthimunki, *can become aggressive when defending their shelters or food.*

Defending your patch

Defending a territory is one way to guarantee your food supply and the larger the territory that you can keep, the more food it will supply.

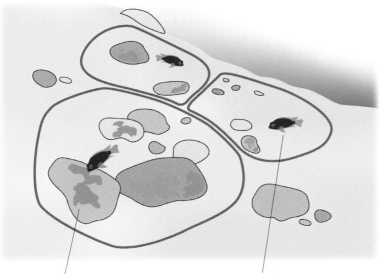

Larger, dominant fish have the edge over their smaller rivals and win the best and largest territories.

Smaller fish have to settle for less, but may trade up as they grow.

Q: How large are fishes' feeding territories?

A: A small territory is easy to defend but does not produce enough food, whereas a large territory produces plenty but is hard to defend. The answer is to opt for a medium-sized one, though the size depends on the competition (more means a smaller territory) and on how good the territory is (the more fertile it is, the smaller it can be).

Q: How do fish defend their food against all the other fish?

A: One important difference between a breeding territory and a feeding territory is that whereas parental fish exert themselves to keep all fish out of their territory, foraging fish save most of their aggression for fish with the same diet as themselves – their main competitors. Research on the shrimp-eating cichlid,

Neolamprologus tetracanthus, showed that territory holders were extremely good at discriminating between different fish and altering the intensity of defense according to the threat posed to the food supplies.

Q: Do fish defend their territories constantly?

A: Territory defence uses up a great deal of a fish's energy, so it only happens when the payback to the fish is high. If the amount of food produced by a territory starts to decline, then the benefit to the fish in defending that territory will also decline and the fish is likely to give it up and move on. This usually happens over a period of days or weeks, but for cichlids in Lake Tanganyika, it happens on a much more regular basis. High levels of sunshine cause algae on the rocks in the shallows of the lake to photosynthesise at peak levels between midday and about 4 pm. This means that the nutritional value of the algae also peaks at this time, making it worthwhile for *Tropheus moori* to defend their own patch between these hours, despite coexisting in foraging groups before noon and after 4 pm.

Breeding territories

A large number of fish species provide care for their young, and for the males of such species, finding a good territory is very often a prerequisite for attracting a mate. Breeding territories usually have much in common with feeding territories; a ready supply of food close to hand is a definite advantage. In addition, a good breeding territory will usually also include some cover to protect the eggs and young. Males choose their sites carefully and, once chosen, defend them vigorously against other males. A well-selected territory will have everything a female could desire and will add considerably to the male's chances of securing a good mate.

Left: Border disputes are common between males with neighboring territories (here Enantiopus) *and these can become especially fierce when females show up.*

Q: Who gets the best territories?

A: The largest, most dominant males usually end up in possession of the best territories because they are prepared to fight for them and are best equipped to win their disputes. The advantage of a good territory is considerable when it comes to getting the opportunity to mate and raise the subsequent fry. Not only do the growing youngsters have more food close to hand, they are also safer from predators than in a poorer territory. Female fish are good judges of territory quality and will reward the efforts of any male who has staked his claim in a good territory by mating with him. With such huge benefits on offer, it is little wonder that males are prepared to fight over the best pitches. But males often pay a high price for their luxury accommodation; the constant fending off of rivals who would steal the territory means they have little time to feed or recuperate and very often have to abandon their prize real estates at some point during the breeding season.

Q: How do lesser males compete for territories?

A: Quite often, the best territories are bordered by a number of others that are slightly less desirable to the fish, but good territories nonetheless. Continuing outwards and away from the peak spot, territories decline in value and these outer plots are held by subordinate males. Thus a kind of mosaic builds up, with large clusters of average territories with average males surrounding the local hotshots in their hard-won super-territories. If a female seeks to mate with the dominant male in his central territory, the satellite males in their more peripheral territories frantically display to her, doing anything to persuade her to remain and lay her eggs.

Occasionally they might succeed, but more often the females give them little encouragement, preferring to spawn with the best possible mates.

Q: How do fish deal with their boundary disputes?

A: Boundary disputes between adjacent territory holders are fascinating affairs. First, one fish adopts a threat posture and charges its neighbor, who in turn backs off. But as they cross the boundary between territories the aggressor loses confidence. The retreating fish, by contrast, gains some steel and charges the other. This leads to a good deal of to-ing and fro-ing at the territory's edge, which is often denoted by some kind of landmark, such as a stone or clump of weed. However, the ceaseless demands of territory defense often cause fish to declare a truce with their immediate neighbors. This fragile non-aggression pact, sometimes called the "dear enemy" effect, enables fish to avoid petty squabbling with the same few neighboring individuals, while allowing them to defend vigorously against outsiders.

Breeding territories in the wild

During the breeding season, patchworks of male breeding territories can cover much of the habitat, with each male frantically displaying to passing females.

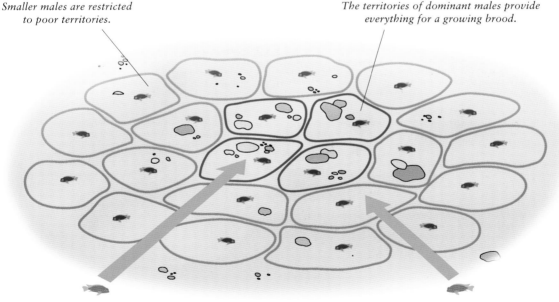

Smaller males are restricted to poor territories.

The territories of dominant males provide everything for a growing brood.

Lesser males often set up home near to the top males' territories, hoping to intercept females.

Females will sometimes mate with a subordinate male, especially if the dominant is unreceptive.

Dominance hierarchies

Although dominance hierarchies were first studied in domestic chickens — hence the term "pecking order" — many different kinds of animals, including fish, fight it out among themselves to see who is boss. In the wild, these dominance hierarchies are usually formed between conspecifics, but in the aquarium a hierarchy can often develop between the inhabitants, regardless of their species.

Q: Why do fish establish dominance hierarchies?

A: Hierarchies develop when individual fish attempt to stake a claim for a share of the resources, which in most cases means food. The largest and most aggressive fish are capable of out-competing others, so they take a disproportionate chunk for themselves, leaving the others to squabble for what is left. Through aggression and direct competition, the fish gradually decide an order of precedence, from the dominant individuals at the top of the hierarchy down to the weaker subordinate fish at the bottom.

Q: How do fish decide on their place in the hierarchy?

A: The most obvious way is for fish to stage a series of contests, involving a great deal of displaying and even out-and-out fighting, but this is by no means the only method they use. Simply by watching others fight, fish can decide whether they have any real chance against the combatants. If they decide that one or other of the fighters is a real bruiser, they can save themselves from injury by signaling submissiveness to these fish in the future. Perhaps the best predictor of a fish's position in a dominance hierarchy is its size, but even among closely matched fish the order is usually established extremely quickly, often within 24 hours.

Q: What happens once the pecking order has been decided?

A: Once every fish knows its place in the hierarchy, and the place of all the others, there is

Left: Settling the issue of who is the boss is top of the agenda for fish that have not encountered one another before, such as these Julidochromis transcriptus.

peace. Actual fighting becomes extremely rare, although dominant fish occasionally nip at their subordinates, just to remind them who is boss. Some amazing work on catfish has shown that after the order has been established, the hierarchy members release what has been called a "peace pheromone" to cement the new harmony. This chemical in the fishes' water decreases further the likelihood of fighting. In fact, if water taken from a tank containing an established hierarchy is poured into one where the fish are battling it out, the fish in the second tank rapidly calm down and pause all aggression.

Q: What happens if a fish is taken out of its hierarchy?

A: If a member of a hierarchy is taken out of its home tank – for example at an aquarium shop – and moved to a new tank where the fish have already formed a hierarchy, its behavior in the new tank will depend on its previous rank. If it was previously a dominant fish, it will fight for a similarly high rank. If it was already towards the bottom of the pecking order, it will very likely have to accept a degree of bullying and a position right at

the bottom of the new hierarchy. Newcomers must contend with home advantage, which is just as much a factor for fights between fish as it is in the sporting world. If a fish is put back into the same

hierarchy after a period of less than a few weeks away, it is likely to slot straight back into its old rank. It will remember its old tankmates and vice versa.

The peace pheromone

Dominance hierarchies are common among fishes. Typically, once the fish have fought it out to determine the order of precedence, calm returns and the fish become much less aggressive.

1 *Fish that are newly introduced to one another frequently fight among themselves to decide who is boss.*

2 *The fighting continues until each individual fish knows its place in the pecking order.*

Flask with water containing the "peace" pheromone.

3 *With the hierarchy established, some fishes produce a pheromone that seems to promote harmony.*

4 *Adding peace pheromone to a tank containing squabbling fish causes them to call a truce.*

Fish fights – the lead-up

Like all animals, fish have to compete to acquire resources such as food, territories, or mates. When the stakes are high, for example during the breeding season, this competition can escalate into direct aggression. But actual fighting is extremely costly – even the victor can sustain serious injuries. Consequently, fish go to great lengths to size up their opposition, trying to scare their rivals and impress them into backing down, while all the time attempting to work out their own chances of winning if it should come to a fight.

Q: How do fish try to scare their rivals?

A: Fish have evolved a number of ways of assessing an opponent's strength without actually coming to blows. Rivals are often seen displaying to one another visually, spreading fins to accentuate size and color, thus demonstrating their condition and potential strength. These might be frontal displays, where the fish are face-to-face, flaring their gill covers at one another, or lateral displays where the fish are side-by-side, either stationary or circling one another, with their bodies held rigid and fins erect.

Q: What do the displays mean?

A: A large fish in good health will almost always beat a smaller rival, which is why fish principally try to accentuate their size during displays. Meanwhile, color is a good indicator of a fish's health, which again will be closely linked to its fighting performance at a particular point in time. Although it is possible for fish to make the most of their color and size using displays, these are two

Aggression on display

1 *These Cuming's barbs adopt a flank-to-flank display, trying to convince each other to back down.*

2 *The fish spread their fins to the greatest extent to emphasise both their size and condition.*

3 *When the fish start to circle one another, it is a sign that an attack may not be far off.*

strength, such as jaw locking, where two fish grip onto each other's mouth and perform a tug-of-war to determine who is the strongest. Although scarcely suspected just a few years ago, it seems very likely that fish frequently use additional signals as a matter of course during their visual displays. Croaking gouramis "growl" at one another, and *Tilapia* back up their visual displays with pulses of urine, using the pheromones that it contains to communicate their strength chemically.

Above: Male Siamese fighting fish (Betta splendens) *flare their unusually large gill covers in an exaggerated display of aggression.*

factors that cannot be faked; a fish cannot pretend to be twice the size it is and it cannot develop strong colours if it is not in the peak of health, so both are honest signals of a fish's quality.

Q: What happens if the visual displays don't work?

A: Although the signals that protagonists send one another are full of bluff and bluster, there has to be a sizeable core of truth within them, because escalating to a fight is bad news for all concerned. However, if two fish are very closely matched in size and color, a series of visual displays may sometimes fail to settle the issue. Even so, a fight can still be avoided. The fish continue to use displays but start to back these up with other signals. Lateral displays are very often supported by each fish sharply contracting its muscles, causing its body to wave and send a pulse of water towards the opponent. This allows each fish to assess very directly its rival's strength via the pressure-sensitive lateral line. Occasionally, the fish conduct more direct tests of

Above: The bright yellow patterns on the fins of forktail rainbowfish (Pseudomugil furcatus) *serve to accentuate their displays.*

Fish fights – coming to blows

Occasionally, if two closely matched fish fail to decide the issue by displaying, an actual fight may develop. However, this is a relatively rare occurrence and the two aggressors must be very closely matched, with a great deal at stake, before they fight.

Q: *What happens in a fish fight?*

A: Although this varies from fish to fish, there are some common threads in all fishy altercations. For one thing, the combatants usually tend to target the same parts of their opponents' bodies.

Top targets are often the fins. This makes sense, because a torn fin is likely to slow down a foe. Any vulnerable part is fair game; fish often attack the eyes and unprotected flanks of their enemies. A full-blown fight rarely lasts longer than a few minutes at most. Once one fish has landed a

Fighting fish

Fish fights tend to follow a clear pattern, from displaying and tussling to fighting before the winner chases off the loser.

Jaw locking allows the fish to directly assess each other's strength without risking injury.

I *Displays are highly ritualized and designed to deter an opponent from further aggression.*

2 *When displays fail to settle the issue, aggression levels can increase rapidly.*

3 *The fight can often be decided in the blink of an eye and one fish turns to flee.*

Fish wounds

Fish fights in the wild seldom result in serious injury to either protagonist, simply because a defeated fish can escape. In the aquarium there is no place to hide. This can result in torn or even missing fins, missing scales and open wounds on a fish's flanks.

few telling blows – or bites – the impulse to fight can rapidly leave the other and it may seek to break contact and flee.

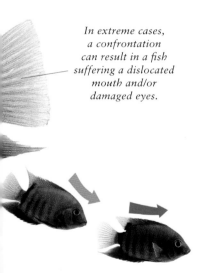

In extreme cases, a confrontation can result in a fish suffering a dislocated mouth and/or damaged eyes.

4 *Victorious fish will seldom tolerate the presence of a beaten rival nearby.*

Q: *How is a winner decided?*

A: It can be hard for a human onlooker to judge which fish is gaining the upper hand in a contest. Moreover, responsible aquarists would most likely be hurrying to separate the fish, rather than settling down to a ringside seat. Although a "two falls or a submission" rule clearly does not exist between fish, the loser seems to realize when the fight is lost. How much damage must be inflicted before this realization occurs can often depend on how much is at stake; fish will risk a great deal more and accept greater injury for a brood of their young than to contest a morsel of food.

Q: *What happens after a fight?*

A: After the victory has been decided the losing fish must make itself scarce, otherwise its life might be at risk. The winner will not tolerate its presence in the immediate area and will continue to attack – no mercy is given. In the open waters of the wild, this is rarely a problem, but in the confines of an aquarium the constant harrying by the victor may prove fatal. Death could occur in the aftermath of the

battle if open wounds become infected; as we have seen, fighting is an extremely costly business. If both fish survive, they are unlikely to fight again. Fish tend to remember the identity of their conquerors and do not make the same mistake twice.

Q: *How do other fish respond to the combatants?*

A: Amazingly, fish are able to weigh up their chances by watching a fight between their rivals. This phenomenon, known as the "bystander effect," has been studied in a number of species, including Siamese fighting fish. The bystanders can gauge their chances against each of the two protagonists and may act on this information by challenging the unfortunate loser of the first fight, or even the winner, afterwards. This behavior allows fish a simple and, for the observers, harmless way of working out whether they might win a fight without actually becoming involved. In fact, even the simple stimulus of watching a fight causes the bystander to become more aggressive and makes it more likely to win a fight against an unsuspecting opponent.

Aggression and stress

It is not only humans that can feel "stressed out." As serene as an aquarium may look, its occupants can suffer from the pressures of day-to-day life. In fish, stress is usually a response to aggressive behavior and can occur whether the fish is the target or the instigator. Fish exposed to extended periods of stress can suffer all kinds of effects, from reductions in growth rate to greater susceptibility to disease. Minimizing the stress that fish suffer is essential to maintaining a healthy aquarium.

Above: Folded fins, as seen in this jaguar cichlid (Parachromis managuensis), *are a classic sign of submission and stress in fishes.*

Q: How can you tell if a fish is stressed?

A: In some circumstances, it is obvious that fish are stressed; they lose color, they lose their appetite, and behave in a generally listless fashion. However, high stress levels can also occur in fish that look and behave perfectly normally. This was discovered by taking blood samples from fish and measuring levels of particular hormones, such as cortisol, which are produced by the body in response to stress.

Q: What do these stress hormones do?

A: The purpose of hormones such as cortisol is to prepare the body for action, to keep the metabolism ready to go into battle. For example, one of the functions of cortisol is to prevent the body from storing its energy reserves, thereby keeping them available for instant use. Extended periods of high stress hormone levels can affect the fish's osmoregulation and reduce the amount of energy that the body puts towards fighting disease.

Q: Which fish get stressed and why?

A: In the home aquarium, any fishes that are involved in aggression – either doling it out or taking it – become stressed. This includes fish that are breeding, fish that are behaving territorially, and fish that are in dominance hierarchies – quite a large group, when you consider it. Levels of stress vary from fish to fish, but cortisol can be especially high in subordinate fish and in fish that spend long periods of time guarding their young.

Q: Do hormones affect the way a fish behaves?

A: Hormones do affect the way a fish behaves and this relates

Above: Chemical cues enable catfish to determine each other's social status: dominant individuals smell different to subordinates.

directly to its social status and also to the way it looks and even smells. Male fish with high levels of blood cortisol and low levels of androgens (male sex hormones) are less likely to display or fight. Catfish can distinguish between dominant and subordinate conspecifics on the basis of their smell; the difference in their odors relate to hormone levels in the body.

Q: Do fish hormones affect the way a fish fights?

A: One fascinating aspect of the aggression that can occur between fishes closely mirrors a phenomenon sometimes seen in human sporting contests. When a male swordtail wins a fight with another male, he gets (in simple terms) a testosterone rush. This rush can last for a few days and makes him much more likely to solicit another fight and, remarkably, also makes him more likely to win. His vanquished opponent suffers by comparison and the defeat makes him more likely to lose subsequent battles. These occurrences, sometimes termed "winner and loser effects," can help lead a fish on to a winning run or a losing streak.

Below: Parental fish suffer considerable stress while guarding their young. They cannot afford to relax their vigilance.

Keeping it in the family

The fish world is not all about fighting; more and more evidence is accumulating of acts of co-operation between fish. One of the most amazing facts is their ability not only to recognize their relations, but also to extend a helping fin when the occasion arises. The ability to recognize kin seems to vary between species, but there are many examples of fish that can recognize not only their own parents or offspring, but also their siblings and even half-siblings.

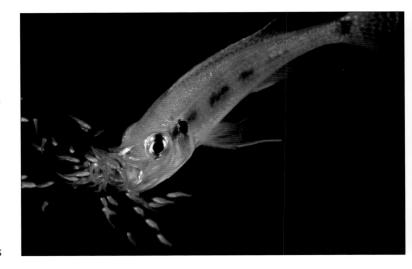

Above: When danger threatens, Haplotaxodon microlepis *fry rush to the safety of their father's mouth. Within moments all will be safely concealed from danger.*

Q: Why would fish co-operate with their relatives?

A: There are good biological reasons why it is a good idea to help a relative if at all possible. As we have seen, each individual fish is on a mission to breed during its lifetime and pass on its genes to the next generation. This urge is an extremely strong one; male guppies risk their lives for it and female mouthbrooders come close to starving themselves to death for their young. As well as breeding, another way of trying to win in life's game is to improve the chances of those that carry your genes; brothers, sisters, parents and offspring all fall into this category.

Q: How do fish know who is a relative and who is not?

A: Fish use two main methods to recognize their relatives. The first is simple and not foolproof: treat those with whom you grow up as your relatives. An experiment neatly showed the flaw in this strategy; single baby guppies were raised with a brood of swordtail fry and it was later shown that the guppies considered themselves to be swordtails! The second method of recognizing your relatives is potentially more tricky but allows for greater accuracy. In this case, fish use smell to discriminate between kith and kin. All individual fish produce a subtle but unique odor. The odors of two related individuals are more similar than those of two unrelated fish, so by comparing the smell of another fish to itself – known as self-referencing – a fish can determine whether the two are related.

Q: How do fish co-operate with their relatives?

A: Research into fish behavior has revealed many different examples of fish aiding their kin. Some seem pretty mild by human standards; for instance, it has been shown that wild parental livebearers prefer not to cannibalize their own fry. Cichlid parents are also able to distinguish between their own and other fry. But some fish can also recognize their siblings. Certain territorial species allow their brothers and sisters access to their territories to feed or to hide, while aggressively defending against unrelated interlopers. In another example, rainbowfish prefer to school with their relatives, and in doing so spread a variety of benefits around the family group. Some cichlids remain at their parental nests to help their parents raise their siblings (see page 180).

Above: Parental mouthbrooders make great sacrifices for their young, often starving themselves.

Below: These Lamprologus caudopunctatus *can distinguish between relatives and strangers.*

A helping fin

Although each fish has to behave selfishly and look out for its own interests, it would be wrong to assume that fish never co-operate. During predator inspection, a pair or a small group of fish co-operate in order to fulfill a task, and there are several other examples. Fish generally co-operate in order to do something they would be unable to achieve alone. By doing so, they increase their own benefits and, as a by-product, increase those of their co-operators – sometimes termed a "win-win" situation. Although the fish are not behaving altruistically in the truest sense of the word, there are cases where co-operation seems to be the basis for long-standing arrangements between fish.

Q: How do fish co-operate?

A: Some tasks are more efficiently carried out in groups than by solitary individuals. The largest single day-to-day task for fish is to fulfill their energy requirements – to gather enough food to maintain themselves and

to grow. Perhaps not surprisingly, one of the first reported instances of co-operation was from a study on sunfish, which choose to associate with co-operative foraging partners, rather than individuals with whom they have had less positive experiences. The Malawi cichlid *Cyrtocara moorii* goes a step further and actually protects its foraging partners. In the wild, *C. moorii* sometimes forages with another cichlid, *Taeniolethrinops praeorbitalis,* which feeds by digging deep into the sand and sieving out the small animals hidden there. This digging behavior disturbs other invertebrates, which *C. moorii*

feeds on. The free lunch that *C. moorii* gets from *T. praeorbitalis* is repaid by the protection it gives its feeding partner.

Q: Are there any fish that gang up to attack?

A: One unusual advantage of living in a group is that it can sometimes allow the individuals in that group to storm into a defended territory and take

Below: Teamwork can sometimes pay for different fish species. Here Cyrtocara moorii *(blue fish) works with its foraging partner* Taeniolethrinops *to mutual benefit.*

the rich pickings available. The algae-eating cichlid *Petrochromis fasciolatus* does precisely this, combining into large groups before launching a raid. The territory owners have little chance when faced with such a mass invasion and have to submit to superior numbers.

Q: Do fish ever co-operate in defense?

A: There is some evidence that different species of cichlids in Lake Tanganyika assist one another in excluding a common enemy from their territories. The two species *Tropheus moorii* and *Petrochromis trewavasae* each defend feeding territories, but their diets are slightly different. Both eat vegetable matter, but in the wild

Above: Tropheus moorii *(right) and* Petrochromis trewavasae *combine to breach the defences of a territory in order to feed on the protected resources within.*

T. moorii's diet also includes a proportion of worms, crustaceans, and insects. The fact that they are not direct rivals for the same resources is perhaps the reason they allow their territories to

overlap. More than this, they seem to join forces to exclude larger cichlids, an unlikely feat without such co-operation.

Q: Do larger fish allow small fish to groom them?

A: Cleaning behavior is well known on the world's tropical marine reefs, but it also occurs in freshwater. The cichlid *Pseudotropheus crabro* cleans parasites from the skin of the large kampango catfish *(Bagrus meridionalis)* in much the same way. However, its apparently innocent intentions were given the lie when it was discovered that the cichlid not only eats the catfish's parasites, but opportunistically, a proportion of the larger fish's eggs as well.

Below: Pseudotropheus crabro *gets food by cleaning parasites from the skin of* Bagrus meridionalis.

Chapter 8
Battle of the sexes

The so-called battle of the sexes is enormously important to the way that fish behave and the way that they look, and it's all down to the unequal costs that the different sexes bear in producing offspring.

Throughout the animal kingdom the interests of males and females are in conflict. For most species this means that males want to mate with as many different females as possible, while females try to avoid unwelcome advances and be more selective about their potential suitors.

Q: Is the cost of breeding equal for males and females?

A: No. The reason for this state of disharmony is at least partly due to a phenomenon known as anisogamy, which simply means "different-sized gametes." Each sex produces sex cells – gametes – that contain genetic information. Male gametes are known as sperm and female sex cells are eggs. Fertilization occurs when the two fuse. The great thing for the male is that sperm cells are tiny in comparison to the eggs they fertilize. This means they require

less energy to produce. What is more, males of most species can produce enough sperm cells to fertilize huge numbers of eggs; in other words, males have the capability to fertilize the eggs of tens, hundreds, even thousands of females, if the chance arises. The more eggs a male fertilizes, the more genes he passes on, so

his strategy in the game of life is to court and cajole as many females as possible in his lifetime. By contrast, females have to invest heavily in their eggs. Each one is packed with nutrients for the developing embryo and comes

Right: A pair of green terrors (Aequidens rivulatus) at close quarters during the latter stages of their courtship.

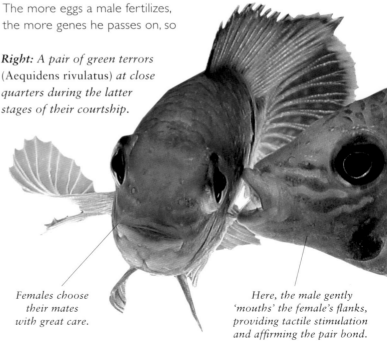

Females choose their mates with great care.

Here, the male gently 'mouths' the female's flanks, providing tactile stimulation and affirming the pair bond.

at a real cost. A female can only produce a finite number of eggs, so it pays her to be choosy and to select the best father for her offspring – the one whose genes will give them the best chance of success in life.

Q: How does this affect fish in the wild?

A: The inequality between the sexes is well illustrated by studies carried out on wild cichlids living in Central America. Research showed that successful males were able to father anything up

to nine separate broods over the course of one breeding season, whereas the females, who invest so much more in the eggs and young, usually only managed one or, rarely, two broods over the same timespan.

Q: How do the different sexes try to win out?

A: As with any struggle, the two sides develop strategies. Females are picky about their partners, so males develop ways of attracting them. These include bright colors, unusual display behavior patterns, and ornamentation – such as the swordtail's sword. But all

is not fair in love and war and many males have developed sneaky ways of circumventing female choice. Males also fight one another for the attentions of females. Although they are not limited by their body's ability to father offspring, their plans are sometimes limited by the presence of other males who have different ideas. Among species that provide parental care, males can be especially aggressive towards one another as they need to defend their territories, their mates and young. Here, we look at the sex war and the fascinating ways that fish have evolved as a consequence.

Above: An amorous male, displaying his vivid breeding colors, intercepts a potential mate and makes his move.

Bright is best

The dazzling colors of many of the fish species available to aquarists are often the result of millions of years of choosy females looking for the perfect mate. A host of different species show sexual dichromatism, meaning that males and females of the same species show dramatically different color patterns. The list includes many of the annual killifish and rainbowfish, as well as the smaller gouramis and the guppy. Males of various other species – especially schooling fish – only show this sexual dichromatism at breeding time, becoming brilliantly colored only when it really counts.

Q: Are there costs of being colorful?

A: Although standing out from the crowd is a great tactic for attracting the attention of impressionable females, it also brings males to the attention of hungry predators. As a result, males face competing pressures. One common response is, in a sense, to hide their light under a bushel. Juvenile males of sexually dichromatic species have nothing

Above: Males are often more colorful than females, as is the case with this vivid male Otopharynx lithobates.

to gain from advertising to females at such an early age and, therefore, are most often identical in appearance to females. Their advertisements are only switched on at the onset of sexual maturity, so male guppies blossom when the time is ripe. Once this change happens, it is a race for the males to be noticed before a predator, such as a pike cichlid that shares their home, notices them. Lifespans for matured male guppies in the stream of their Trinidadian home can be measured in days – the added

conspicuousness of their breeding livery is a huge cost to bear. In streams where many predators are present, mature male fish are far less colorful than in those where predators are few and far between. This reflects the balance that males must strike between the competing pressures of mating against surviving. The same applies to the huge numbers of fish species whose adult males color up only during the breeding season. Although aquarists might prefer male fish to maintain their vivid colors on a permanent basis, there are sound reasons in the fishes' evolutionary history to explain why this should not be so.

Q: Do male colors attract aggression from other males?

A: Yes. Bright male coloration not only attracts predators, but also excites the fury of other males. The stripe patterns of paternal convict cichlids become especially vivid during the breeding season and it is a basic truism that the bolder the stripes, the bolder the male. In fact, males reserve most of their aggression for the most boldly striped competitors.

Q: Can a male display be fatal?

A: In addition to the costs already mentioned, there are also energetic costs for the males in developing their rich hues. The metabolic effort invested in creating their breeding garb can often result in a weakened immune system, which can lead to a fish acquiring diseases and parasites. In some species, the

Above: In the breeding season, male cherry barbs (Barbus titteya) *adopt the breeding colours for which the species is named.*

Below: The cherry red belly of the female krib (Pelvicachromis *spp.*) *signals her readiness to breed.*

effort required to spruce up can contribute to an early death.

Q: Do females ever use bright breeding colors?

A: There are some examples of males being choosy, based on the colors of females. One possible example is the krib, where females develop bright red bellies during the breeding season. There are suggestions that this may accentuate the males' perception of the roundness of the females' egg-filled bellies and their readiness to breed.

Sexy sons and discerning daughters

So how does a female fish decide what makes for a good mate and what are the benefits to her of being picky? One idea suggests that by homing in on a particular male trait – be it color or ornamentation – the females of any given species help to bring about a kind of evolutionary spiral. After a successful mating, the female passes on her genes to her daughters. Included in the genetic package are the very genes that predisposed the mother to choose the male trait. This means that her

daughters are more likely to be born with a preference for a similar type of male to their father. So if the female preferred, say, a bright red male, then her daughters will grow up to go weak at the fins for bright red males. At the same time, the female

benefits because her sons will gain their father's genes and, she hopes, be bright red just like him. Therefore, when they grow up, they should be successful in attracting mates too. In this way, female choice produces sexy sons and discerning daughters and, with them, her best chance for genetic immortality.

The comparatively drab female chooses her mate.

The male sailfin molly puts on a stunning courtship display.

Q: How far can these male traits develop?

A: Once species become locked into this loop, over time, males with more exaggerated traits and females with an ever-greater desire to respond to them are produced. If this loop was not held in check, we might, for example, expect to see male sailfin mollies with dorsal fins the size of handkerchiefs. The fact that this is not the case is down to the costs to the male. They would be too great, in terms of the energetic costs of producing them and the handicap they would cause when swimming or escaping a predator. Thus, the spiral of exaggerated ornamentation and colors is limited.

Q: Do the signals have anything to do with the real quality of a male?

A: In many cases the male color or ornament can reveal the quality of the male. Only those males that forage well and have good immune systems are able to produce the really bright colors or the most dramatic ornaments. The extreme cost to the male of producing a really first-class display means he has to be in top shape, signaling to the female that he has excellent genes and is a worthy father for her offspring.

Q: What about species that have almost identical males and females?

A: Of course, not all fish display dramatic sexual dimorphism or dichromatism. In some species the sexes can be incredibly difficult to tell apart, even to a trained eye. This is especially the case in many schooling fish, where to stand out from the crowd is a sure way to end up as lunch. Not only that, but many schooling fishes breed in larger groups, so the female has comparatively little choice over

who fathers her offspring. There is little advantage to the male in being showy – better for him that he should be quick instead.

Below: This wild male swordtail (Xiphophorus montezumae) has not only a vivid sword, but also an impressive dorsal fin.

Above: Typically of schooling fishes, silver sharks (Balantiocheilos melanopterus) show almost no differences between males and females – to a human eye, at least!

Q: Do females ever copy one another's choices?

A: One way for a female to make sure she is selecting the best possible male is to see who other females choose. Female mollies are known to mimic the choices of other females and show a strong tendency to mate with the local hotshot. The same patterns are also shown in egg-laying species, where the male guards the nest. Females of a number of different species have been shown to seek out and lay their eggs in nests that already contain the eggs of other females.

Extras fitted as standard

Brightly colored males just do not quite cut the mustard for females of some fish species. Instead, they prefer to use some other trait to compare and discriminate between prospective mates. Again, female choice has been the driving force behind the evolution of an incredible diversity of male so-called "ornaments." From the sword of the swordtail, and the sail of the sailfin molly to the bristles of the bristlemouth catfish, males of many different species are decked out with all manner of unusual appendages. These are very seldom functional in any sense – quite the opposite in most cases – except as a means of attracting the female of the species.

Q: What examples of male ornaments are there in the fish world?

A: There are often fairly obvious morphological means of distinguishing between the male and female fish. The male pearl

Pearl gouramis show both color and morphological differences between the sexes. These are largely driven by female choice.

gourami (Trichogaster leeri) has threadlike extensions to his anal fin. Male spotted corys (Corydoras punctatus) have longer and thicker pectoral fins than females. Many male cyprinids develop a rash of breeding tubercules over their

heads at certain times of year, and so on. The primary – and in some cases, sole – purpose of these ornaments is to attract females.

Q: What is the swordtail's secret of success?

A: For a male swordtail, the extended and colored rays at the bottom of the caudal fin can be his passport to success, if they are sufficiently dramatic to impress the females. Experiments using these fish have shown the importance placed by females on the male's sword. Researchers have shown that when given a choice between a male with a long and vividly colored sword and a male with a less impressive sword, they opt for the former. But when the second male is provided with a prosthetic sword – a piece of bright plastic attached to the tail – they switch their preference and are won over by his new-found style.

Left: The male swordtail's sword is used by females as a measure of his quality as a potential mate and father to her offspring.

Q: What are the bristles of the bristlenose catfish used for?

A: One of the most dramatic examples of ornamentation in male fish can be seen in male bristlenose catfish *(Ancistrus spp.)*. Juvenile fish possess short fleshy bristles around the mouth, but with the onset of sexual maturity, these grow to dramatic proportions. However, in this case the "signal" may have evolved

to fool the females. *Ancistrus* species lay their eggs in nests, guarded by the males. When they have a choice, females prefer to spawn in nests where the male is already guarding eggs; they respond to mate selections made by earlier females. But how do you encourage a female to be the first to lay her eggs in your

nest? There are some suggestions that the male's bristles mimic the presence of fry in the nest, fooling the female into thinking that the male is already in charge of one of more broods and will therefore make a good parent for her offspring. One supporting piece of evidence for this is that the bristles are approximately the same size and shade as larval *Ancistrus* at an early stage in their development.

Below: Male Ancistrus catfish have a remarkable set of "whiskers" whose sole purpose is to attract females by one means or another.

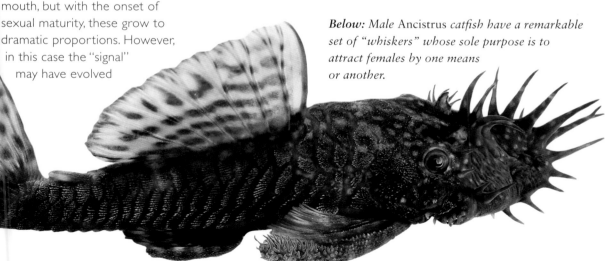

Size matters

One unusual feature of fish, especially when compared to mammals and birds, is the way that adults can vary so enormously in size. Female platies (Xiphophorus maculatus) can produce offspring when less than 1 inch (2.5 cm) long, but can grow to reach over twice this size, especially if they do not mate when young. Similarly, some male cichlids are able to father broods at less than one-third their full adult size. However, the larger a fish, the older it is and the more successful it has been during its life at finding food and avoiding predators. As a result, fish often use the size of a prospective partner as a criterion for choosing them.

Q: Why do some species have larger males than females when it's the opposite way round in others?

A: The sometimes quite dramatic difference between the sizes of fully grown adults is another unusual thing about fish. In some species, the male dwarfs the female, in others, the reverse is true. The reasons behind this point to the mating system of the species in question, but as a general rule, males that defend territories or that provide parental care tend to be the larger sex, whereas in all others the sexes are either identical in size, or the female is larger.

Q: What are the advantages to a female in being large?

A: The larger the female, the more offspring she can produce and, often, the healthier the eggs and young. This is simply because larger fish have not only size on their side, but also greater energy reserves. Male livebearers are among the smallest of fish in relation to females; for example, male mosquitofish (Heterandria formosa) reach only about half the length of the females. But this does not concern them. As far as a male mosquitofish is concerned, big is beautiful and if given a choice he will devote his attention to the largest female he can find in the knowledge that, if he is successful, she will be able

Above and right: The female mosquitofish (Heterandria formosa) *is enormous in comparison to her mate. Her greater size enables her to produce larger broods. Males actively seek out large females.*

Q: What's the biggest difference between the sexes in a single species?

A: A dramatic example of sexual size dimorphism occurs amongst the shell-dwelling cichlids of Lake Tanganyika. Male *Lamprologus callipterus* can be more than ten times the size of females. One of the main reasons lies in the way the fish breed. Females lay their eggs in the empty shells of aquatic snails and remain inside the shell tending to their brood for considerable periods. Being large would be a disadvantage in terms of being able to fit into the shell. Males, on the other hand, have to be large enough to collect these shells in their mouths and deliver them to their territory.

to produce more offspring than her smaller sisters. In fact, it is not only livebearers that prefer large females; males of most species operate a "the bigger the better" policy for the same reason.

Q: What are the advantages to a male in being large?

A: Being large is an absolute necessity for fish that defend breeding territories. There is a good correlation between the size of a male and the quality of his territory. What is more, if the male stays around to help guard the fry during their vulnerable early stages, his size provides a very effective deterrent to passing predators. The largest males, therefore, provide the females with the best possible chance of

Above: In many fish there are almost no size differences between the sexes – neither gender gains any advantage through size.

successfully raising large numbers of fry. In such species, females given the choice almost always spawn with the largest available male – and sometimes with the largest unavailable one!

Below: The male Lamprologus callipterus *dwarfs his mate, whose size is limited by shell dwelling.*

Fight for the right

Sometimes, if you want something badly enough you have to fight for it, and so it is with fish. For most male fish a perfect world would be one in which he was the only male among a cast of thousands. The reverse is true to an extent in species where the male provides some parental care. Unfortunately for them, it is an imperfect world in this context. Just how imperfect depends on something known as the operational sex ratio (OSR), which is simply the number of available, mature males in comparison to the number of available, mature females in the local environment. Where the OSR is skewed in favor of one sex or the other, violence can erupt between members of the most numerous sex. In some species, including livebearers and characins, mature males inhibit the development of younger males with pheromones, thereby cutting their competition.

Q: Why do my male platies sometimes fight?

A: The platy (Xiphophorus maculatus) is a popular and very peaceful fish found in many community aquariums. But in some circumstances, its quiet disposition can give way to outright aggression. When the OSR in an aquarium is skewed towards males, i.e. when there are more males than females, the males will very often fight among themselves to gain access to a female. Having established who is boss in this way, the dominant male has a much greater chance of mating, whereas his subordinate counterparts must give way. Such aggression can be distressing for the aquarist but is easy to resolve – simply alter the OSR, in this case by adding more females,

War and peace

The likelihood of males fighting is increased enormously when there are not enough females to go around and the males have to vie for their affections.

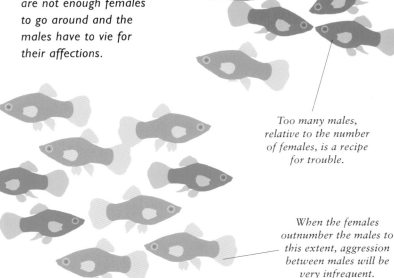

Too many males, relative to the number of females, is a recipe for trouble.

When the females outnumber the males to this extent, aggression between males will be very infrequent.

Q: Why are male fighting fish so aggressive towards other males?

A: More extreme than the platies are the Siamese fighting fish *(Betta splendens)*, which will not tolerate the presence nearby of any male, regardless of how many females are present. One reason lies in their short lifespan; in the wild, fighting fish seldom live longer than one year, meaning they have only one breeding season – one shot at genetic immortality through their fry. Having constructed a bubblenest, the male attempts to persuade as many females as possible to mate. Tenderly, he catches any stray eggs and transfers them to his nest before driving off spent

making sure that they outnumber the quarrelsome males.

Above: Otherwise peaceful, male platies can become extremely feisty when there are too few females to go around.

females. Any males in the area are a threat, both to the paternity of his eggs and their survival; given a chance they are likely to snack on the eggs and fry. With so much at stake, perhaps it is little wonder that they are so aggressive.

Q: Do females ever fight?

A: Although aggression of this kind is more common between male fish, females may also go on the attack in some circumstances. Having paired with a male, female convict cichlids are extremely aggressive to other females, both immediately before and after laying eggs. Interlopers pose a twofold threat: they may eat the eggs and young, but they may also compete for the male's attention, possibly even inducing him to abandon his first brood and set up home with them. This latter threat is what fires up the female, and this is born out by the comparatively half-hearted aggression shown by the males to invading females. Research has shown that female convict cichlids reserve most of their fury in this context for nearby females showing brightly colored bellies, which clearly indicate their readiness to breed.

Left: Male Siamese fighting fish are tender fathers, yet are hyper-aggressive to the presence of other males.

Choosing mates

Humans are highly visual creatures. Sight is our dominant sense and, possibly as a result of this, early research into animal behavior was heavily biased towards the visual signals that pass between creatures. However, comparatively recently, scientists have discovered that fish use a host of amazing and novel means to choose between potential mates.

Q: *How can a female check that she's getting the best male?*

A: When a female fish chooses a mate, she must be sure to pick the best one in order to give her young the greatest chance in life. One especially important consideration is the healthiness of her offspring. The better their immune system, the better equipped they will be to resist infections and diseases. Although this makes sense, it would seem a difficult thing to be able to do; how does the choice of mate affect the offspring's health? Part of the genetic code present in all animals is responsible for building their immune system. In fishes, the genes that perform this job are collectively known as the major histocompatibility complex, or MHC. The best disease resistance is provided by a wide spectrum of MHC genes. The broader the spectrum the better, because this will provide resistance against the widest range of diseases. If a female can find a mate with a different range of MHC genes to

Above: In the clamor and confusion of a mbuna community, selecting a mate of the right species and with all the right qualities must be extremely tricky!

her own, her young will inherit a diverse immune system from both parents. To help with the choice, females can smell prospective mates; MHC genes not only code

for the immune system, but also affect the way each individual smells. So by following her nose, a mother fish makes an extremely important contribution to her offspring's health. Interestingly, humans are also capable of this, though to a lesser extent, so if someone smells good...!

Q: *What's the strangest thing a male does to attract females?*

A: When male Mozambique tilapia *(Oreochromis mossambicus)* smell the presence of a fertile female nearby, they urinate.

On further investigation this apparently strange response makes good sense. The male's urine contains a cocktail of chemicals, most important of which are pheromones that tell the female about the male's social status. The pheromones of dominant males produce a stronger response in their potential mates than the pheromones of subordinate males. The males also use this technique to communicate their social status to other males during aggressive encounters to show who is boss.

Q: *Do fish use any other means to attract the opposite sex?*

A: Many fish also use sound to attract mates. Studies on the cichlids of Lake Malawi have shown that different species produce pulses of sounds during their courtship displays to attract mates. Not only this, but as with songbirds, each species has a slightly different call, specific to its own type. That these calls are used as mating signals is supported by the fact that males also increase their "singing" efforts when a female is nearby.

Picking the perfect partner

The aim of any fish parent is to produce strong and healthy offspring and this can be achieved by avoiding inbreeding. Here, a female gourami (yellow) visits potential male suitors (orange and purple) to assess their genetic suitability as mates.

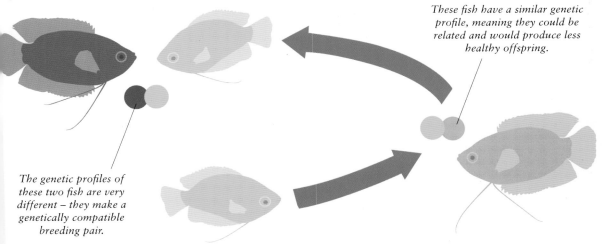

These fish have a similar genetic profile, meaning they could be related and would produce less healthy offspring.

The genetic profiles of these two fish are very different – they make a genetically compatible breeding pair.

Alternative strategies

It is true to say that fish have evolved a number of tactics to cheat the system when the odds are stacked against them, and this is never more true than when the breeding season comes around. The strong and logical preference of both male and female fish for the perfect partner results in inequality. For example, on page 151 we saw how during the breeding season, female cichlids in Central America managed one or two broods, while some males fathered as many as nine. Even if you allow for females producing two broods each, it still means that these hotshot males get more than four times their fair share of matings and, by extension, that quite a few males have missed out. So what is a fish to do if it keeps being overlooked as a mate? Does it simply accept its fate or does it change tactics and become a cheat? As we shall see, the answer is quite definitely the latter.

Q: What are the options for mediocre males?

A: With females putting such a premium on large or showy males, smaller and duller males are often overlooked. This situation can resolve itself among species that form pair bonds, as lower-quality fish take correspondingly lower-quality mates. At other times, males adopt some devious tactics to overcome their natural disadvantages. Female guppies prefer brightly colored males who carry out elaborate displays to woo them into mating. But a proportion of the males in the wild use another strategy. These males, known as "sneaks," are often small and comparatively dull in color. They have no need for the showy colors of their more elegant brothers and instead rely on speed and stealth to sneak in under the female's guard and carry out a kind of "hit-and-run" mating without any courtship. Some nest-making males use similar tactics; smaller males have little chance of establishing their own breeding territory, so instead they set themselves up as satellites to the nest of a larger male. These males, which are often the same size and color as the females, wait until a female enters the dominant male's nest

Left: Resident male territory holders cannot relax their vigilance against small, opportunistic males. This "sneak" Apistogramma diplotaenia *displays to a female.*

to spawn before sneaking in themselves and releasing sperm. Although the territory holder may spot these sneaks and chase them off, it is often too late and a proportion of the female's eggs will have been fertilized by them.

Q: How do female livebearers play the system?

A: Another strategy that females sometimes adopt to make sure they get the best possible young is seen among livebearers. An unmated female will often mate with any reasonable male, possibly because of the potential cost of not mating at all and producing no offspring whatsoever. But after this first mating, the female keeps becoming pickier with each successive suitor, until finally she will accept only the best males. Livebearer broods often have multiple fathers, and research has shown that this actually produces healthier fry – another benefit of playing the field.

Right: If male guppies fail to win the approval of the females through courtship, then they may adopt "sneaky" tactics to catch females unaware.

Playing the field

Like any other female fish, female guppies want to mate with the best males, but it would be a dangerous strategy to hold out for Mr. Right!

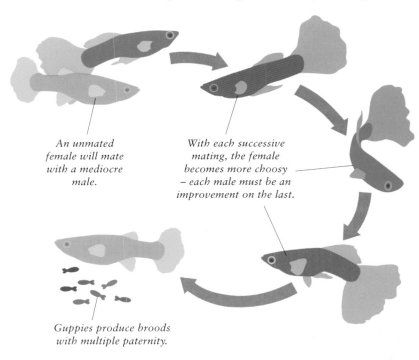

An unmated female will mate with a mediocre male.

With each successive mating, the female becomes more choosy – each male must be an improvement on the last.

Guppies produce broods with multiple paternity.

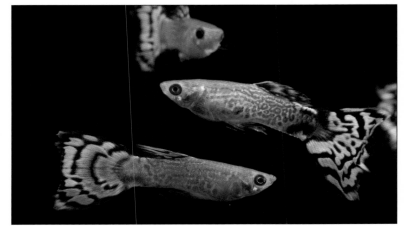

Chapter 9
Fish mating systems

The question of how best to ensure the survival of your offspring so that they carry on the genetic line is a crucial one for all animals, but it has many different "correct" answers, as fish demonstrate.

Fish show an amazing variety of behavior patterns in almost every aspect of their lives, but this is never more true than in the context of reproduction. Most, but not all, animals need two parents (parthenogenetic and hermaphroditic fish exist), but beyond this almost anything goes. Fish use every type of breeding method, from a haphazard scattering of eggs to nurturing their young internally during the most vulnerable stages.

be divided according to whether they provide any parental care. About 80% of fish species provide no direct parental care, but whereas some species simply scatter their eggs on the water currents, others secrete them in safe hiding places. Species that do provide parental care are divided into those where one parent provides the care, including livebearers and mouthbrooders, and those where both parents – and sometimes even a whole family – look after the young.

Above: Nests come in all shapes and sizes, but none are more carefully constructed than the bubblenests of many gouramis.

Q: How many kinds of breeding behavior do fish show?

A: Fish show a huge range of breeding behaviors, from the carefree species that provide no parental care to the doting parents who guard their offspring for weeks. The full spectrum is represented among the popular freshwater aquarium fish species although broadly speaking, fish can

Q: Why do different species that live in the same habitat use such different spawning methods?

A: The critical thing to remember is that what may work for one species may not work for another. Only a tiny fraction of young are likely to survive in any situation, but evolution will favor anything that gives the young

an edge. The critical question for parental fish is whether to produce large numbers of eggs and leave them to fend for themselves or invest energy in guarding fewer eggs. Species tend to settle on the method that, over their evolutionary history, produces the most offspring for them. So while the methods employed by neon tetras and angelfish may be very different, each works well. Defending young may be difficult for small fish, such as neon tetras, so they produce large numbers of young that can disperse when the rivers expand over the floodplains, whereas angelfish are larger and more capable of guarding their fry during their vulnerable stages.

Q: *How do "parental" species decide how much effort to put into raising their young?*

A: The amount of care that each species provides for its young may vary according to the risk that the young face, so where there is little risk, fish may reduce their care. Perhaps surprisingly, some species switch much of their attention to producing as

many young as possible when times are hard. It seems that if parental fish experience unusually harsh conditions, they try to ensure that at least some of their young may survive until things ease up, even if they might not.

Below: Discus (Symphysodon spp.) make excellent parents and invest heavily in each brood to maximize the chances of survival for each of their offspring.

Standard spawning

The vast majority of fish species provide no care for their eggs or young. Many of these species engage in scatter-spawning; in other words, they breed simply by releasing their eggs and sperm into the water column in close proximity and letting nature do the rest.

Q: Isn't this wasteful?

A: In one way, yes, but the parent fish are entirely free of the extra burdens faced by the so-called "caring" species. Unfettered by any consideration other than the costs of producing eggs and sperm, scatter-spawning species can produce huge numbers of fertilized eggs in their spawning bouts, each one a ticket in life's lottery. The fate of the overwhelming majority will be to be eaten, but a tiny proportion always survives to form the next generation.

Q: What are the benefits of scatter-spawning?

A: The energy fish save from not providing care can be diverted to producing large numbers of eggs. A Congo tetra produces 300 to 500 eggs per spawning effort, while a similarly sized fish that provides parental care, such as a dwarf cichlid, may produce a batch of around 100.

Q: What kinds of fish use scatter-spawning?

A: Guarding eggs successfully against all manner of aggressors is no picnic. It is likely to be especially difficult for smaller fish, or those that live in open water, or those that live with large numbers of other fish, all of which are potential egg-predators. Another set of fish that tend to use scatter-spawning almost exclusively are schooling fish. For them, the costs of leaving the safety of the school for a protracted period of childcare are extremely high. When the likelihood of being a successful guardian is small, fish stand to gain very little by performing this role. Better by far for these species to produce plenty of eggs and leave them to it.

Below: A pair of glowlight tetras break apart following the release of sperm and eggs. Getting up close maximizes the number of eggs that are successfully fertilized.

Q: *How do scatter-spawning species mate?*

A: During the breeding season, males display to gravid females ("gravid" meaning heavy with eggs). If the courtship is successful, both fish swim to a spawning site, often a patch of weed, and while locked in an embrace, simultaneously release eggs and sperm. Very often, additional fish, particularly males, accompany the spawning pair, all trying to get in on the act. This can sometimes mean that large numbers of fish form a spawning aggregation. The spawning pheromones released by the breeding adults attract not only conspecifics to the melee but also egg-predators, alerted inadvertently to the feast.

Above: *A male cherry barb nudges a female's egg-swollen belly, in an attempt to encourage her to spawn.*

Left: *The male remains close by, displaying intense breeding colors as part of his diligent courtship.*

Q: *How is paternity decided?*

A: It is of critical importance to each male to fertilize as many eggs as possible. This is why extra males tag along with breeding pairs. Fertilization in scatter-spawning species takes place out in the open water where egg and sperm meet, so to have a chance of fathering the offspring, more than one male may release sperm at the point where the female sheds her eggs. What is more, males adjust the amount of sperm they produce according to the number of rivals in the area, releasing up to six times more when there is plenty of competition compared to when they are alone. In addition, males of many characin species have tiny hooks on the fringes of their anal fins that may be used to hold the female closer during the release of eggs. Some characin species go a step further and use internal fertilization, the male impregnating the female before she releases her eggs.

Above: *Once the female has decided to spawn, the pair align themselves so that sperm and eggs can be released together.*

169

Spreading the risk

Scatter-spawning is the dominant tactic among fish, which hints at its effectiveness; if no fry ever survived, scatter-spawning would be very quickly abandoned as a tactic. That said, it can also be extremely wasteful – only a fraction of one percent of all the eggs produced will ever grow to adulthood – but the parents can take steps that might swing the odds in their favour in this fishy lottery.

Above: Thick clumps of weed, such as this Java moss, provide an excellent spawning site, offering comparative safety for the eggs.

Q: Do these fish just scatter their eggs anywhere?

A: Even though scatter-spawning looks like a careless way of seeding the next generation, the parents do generally take care where they spawn. For example, most species release their sinking eggs close to the substrate, meaning they have less distance to drift in the water column, where they are especially at risk. Many species, including barbs and tetras, spawn in plant thickets, placing their eggs out of the direct view of their most threatening potential predators. Also, when they have a choice, parents head for plants such as mosses and fine-leaved

Cabomba, which provide the maximum protection and are also home to the tiny animals that will comprise the newly hatched fry's diet.

Q: How else can adult fish give their offspring the best chance in life?

A: One of the main things they do is to time their breeding season to coincide with the seasonal upsurge in available food (see page 56). As well as this, some fishes produce adhesive

eggs that attach to plants or underwater structures, which prevents them being washed away in a current or drifting vulnerably around the habitat.

Q: Are fishes' eggs all the same?

A: Definitely not – fish eggs are almost as variable as the fish that lay them. As well as the basic rule that larger fish produce larger eggs, the way each species spawns affects the amount of energy that females put into each egg. The eggs of scatter-spawners are smaller than the eggs of mouthbrooders, but even beyond this there are differences. Female fish will release more eggs when they are courted by a top-class male that they judge to be particularly attractive, than when they are pursued by a lesser male. The amount of energy the female puts into each egg also depends on her condition. If food is plentiful and she is in good shape, each egg that she produces benefits by being better provisioned.

Q: *What happens to the egg?*

A: Life begins in open water, but for most, ends soon after in the jaws of a hungry fish, sometimes in the jaws of their own parents. If it is lucky, the egg will land in a safe spot and begin to develop rapidly before hatching. The eggs of scatter-spawning fish develop and hatch much more quickly than those of species that provide parental care. For example, the eggs of cherry barbs hatch in under two days – about one tenth of the time it takes some mbuna eggs to hatch. Another interesting fact about the newly hatched larvae is that, unlike the larvae of parental species, they do not wriggle while they absorb the yolk sac; keeping very still is a good tactic when you are small and alone.

Egg survival strategies

The aquatic habitat offers plenty of places for eggs to be concealed from their abundant predators, shifting the scales just slightly in favor of their survival.

Right: When fish spawn over gravel, the eggs may fall to safety in the gaps between the stones.

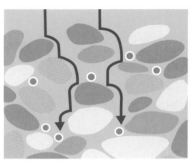

Above: Eggs on the underside of aquatic plant leaves are hopefully out of sight of predators.

Above: Many fish lay sticky eggs that adhere to plants even in a current, which keeps them aerated.

Above: Eggs laid on stones may seem exposed, but are safe from invertebrates in the substrate.

Above: Newly hatched fry cannot swim against a strong current, but seek refuge in the lee of stones.

Placing the eggs

Scatter-spawning can be a risky tactic for fishes that live in flowing water – any eggs that escape being eaten may be simply washed away with the current. By contrast, placing your eggs not only prevents them being swept out of the habitat with the flow, but can also play a part in keeping them safe from predators. Many species of *Corydoras* catfish live in flowing waters and exhibit this egg-placing behavior.

Q: How are the eggs fertilized?

A: Perhaps the most amazing thing about *Corydoras* spawning behavior is the extremely unusual way in which the eggs are fertilized. Studies on the bronze cory show that although the female may be courted by several males, she accepts the advances of only one. The pair form a stereotypical "T" position, with the female's head pressing against the middle of the male's flank. The pressure on the male's flank stimulates him to release sperm which, amazingly, the female catches in her mouth and swallows. The sperm pass through

Spawning, Corydoras style

Corydoras use a unique – but highly effective – method of egg fertilization. It is so unusual, in fact, that it has only recently been conclusively proven.

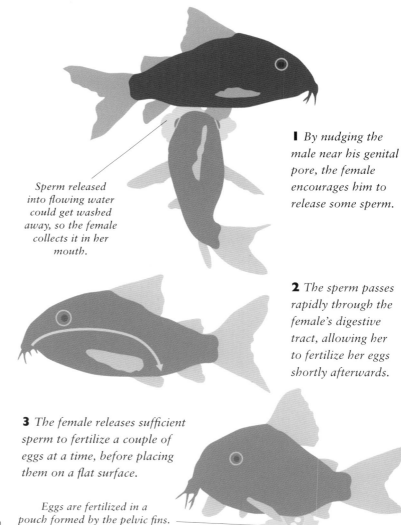

Sperm released into flowing water could get washed away, so the female collects it in her mouth.

1 *By nudging the male near his genital pore, the female encourages him to release some sperm.*

2 *The sperm passes rapidly through the female's digestive tract, allowing her to fertilize her eggs shortly afterwards.*

3 *The female releases sufficient sperm to fertilize a couple of eggs at a time, before placing them on a flat surface.*

Eggs are fertilized in a pouch formed by the pelvic fins.

Above: Peppered corydoras and their relatives seek smooth flat surfaces to lay their eggs. In a tank, this often means the glass!

the female's body and are used by her to fertilize the eggs, which she lays one or two at a time, along with sperm discharged from her intestine, capturing them all in a pouch formed from her pelvic fins. Other species of *Corydoras* also form this "T" position and some, such as the panda cory, carry out the maneuvers in midwater.

Q: How do the sperm survive going through the female's body?

A: Until the publication of a recent study on this bizarre method of fertilization, people had many ideas about how male corys managed to fertilize the eggs. Even now it is not known for sure, but it seems that the ability of corys to breathe by swallowing air and absorbing it through their intestines means that they are also capable of swallowing delicate sperm and passing them quickly and safely through their bodies. It is not known exactly why the catfish perform this unusual behavior, but one credible idea is that in the turbulent streams in which they live, it prevents sperm from being washed away and eggs being left unfertilized.

Q: What does the female do with the fertilized egg?

A: With a fertilized egg in her pelvic fin pouch, the female swims off to seek a good laying site. Sometimes she lays the egg on fine-leaved vegetation, at other times on stones or even the aquarium glass. As she does so, the female is often accompanied by a posse of males, each doubtless hoping to be chosen as her mate to fertilize her next egg. This period of spawning can last several hours, during which time the female may lay between 20 and 40 eggs.

Q: How do the eggs stay attached?

A: *Corydoras* eggs are extremely unusual. They are covered in hexagonal filaments that stick fast to any surface. The filaments can lengthen but will not usually break, making the eggs exceptionally sticky when they are first laid – enough to resist the fast water currents that might otherwise wash them away.

Placing the eggs

Placing the eggs is a kind of compromise strategy between scattering them and providing parental care, but some species tip the balance slightly in favor of their offspring by hiding their eggs in the most ingenious places. As a general rule, scatter-spawning fish gather in large breeding aggregations of many males with one or more females, whereas egg-placing fish usually breed in pairs because the act of spawning requires some co-ordination.

Q: *Where do fish place their eggs?*

A: The ideal spot is obviously out of sight, one where the eggs can develop and hatch before coming to the attention of a voracious predator. But there is quite a lot of variation in the places that fish choose to try to conceal their eggs. Annual killifish dig their eggs deep into the substrate, where they are safe not only from cannibalistic attacks but also from desiccating heat when the temporary pool evaporates. Harlequin rasboras lay their eggs on the underside of broad plant leaves, while

splashing tetras take things a step further and lay their eggs out of the water on overhanging vegetation. *Brycon* characins also leave the water, in a less spectacular but equally effective way, spawning at the splash zone of their home streams, just

above the water line. However, the prize for the most ingenious hiding place for newly laid eggs probably goes to bitterling, which lay their eggs inside the mantle cavity of freshwater mussels, where they are completely safe from all the usual egg-predators.

Above: A pair of killifish prepare to spawn. Their eggs will be safely buried in the substrate.

Left: A pair of harlequin rasboras performing underwater acrobatics to deposit their eggs on the underside of a leaf.

Q: What adaptations do the fish have to enable them to place their eggs?

A: Most egg-placing species have something in common — highly adhesive eggs. It would obviously be a waste of time for the parents to take time choosing a good place for eggs if they did not stick there afterwards. Another common factor among these fishes is their courtships, which tend to be more protracted than those of scattering species.

In harlequin rasboras, the male wraps his body around the female's and it is believed that the pressure of his tail on her abdomen stimulates her to lay eggs. Pairs of splashing tetras have to be highly co-ordinated as they leap from the water to lay their eggs on an overhanging leaf. They jump together, with fins interlocked, and are held

Below: A pair of splashing tetras spawn on a leaf above the surface. The male keeps the eggs moist.

on the leaf for a brief period by the male's suckerlike pelvic fins, while the female lays her eggs and the male fertilizes them. Female bitterlings have evolved an enormously long ovipositor — essentially a tube down which the eggs travel. The ovipositor, which may be considerably longer than the female herself, is guided into the exhalant siphon of the mussel and the eggs are laid safely into their shellfish crib.

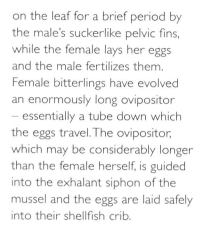

Q: Why do the fish take such care over where they place their eggs?

A: The main reason for carefully choosing spawning sites is to reduce the risk that each egg faces of being eaten before it even hatches. By doing this, the female can afford to lay fewer eggs and therefore saves considerable energy. The downside to this strategy is that these species only lay a few eggs at a time, so spawning tends to take much longer. This not only cuts into the amount of time available to the fish for foraging, but also exposes them to much greater risk of being eaten. Spawning fish are not great multi-taskers and with their vigilance reduced, can often fall prey to an opportune predator.

Staying home for the kids

About one in every five species of fish provides care for the eggs and young. In most cases — something like 75% — the care is provided by only one parent. Looking after the young is expensive, as any human parent will testify, although the costs that fish suffer are rather different. Looking after the young usually ties the parent fish to a particular place, makes it more conspicuous to predators and distracts its attention from potential threats. Parental cichlids have been shown to be at far greater risk of being eaten by birds than other, non-guarding fish in the same population. Another cost faced by the parents is that of lost opportunities — guarding one brood of young usually means that, for the time being, the parent cannot breed again.

Q: If only one parent guards the young is it usually the mother or the father?

A: In most cases the male fish guards the young. One suggested reason is that males must stay to fertilize the eggs after the female

has laid them, giving the female an opportunity to escape and leave the male "holding the babies." As we have seen (page 150), the cost of producing gametes is higher for females than for males — eggs are larger than the sperm that fertilize them — so the females may need a period of recuperation rather than an extended period of guarding. To balance this out, a male fish often tries to attract several females to spawn in his nest, which increases the benefit he gets out of guarding. Genetic analysis has shown that in the nests of some wild male gouramis, up to eleven separate females had

laid eggs. The downside is that, in some instances, new females laying at the nest eat some of the eggs of earlier partners as they spawn.

Q: What's in it for the guarding parent?

A: Given the costs of guarding young, it is perhaps surprising that a lone parent guards at all. The reason they do is that, on

Below: Guarding males, such as this Sturisoma aureum, *often have the eggs of more than one female (here pale and dark) in their nest.*

Above: A male firemouth cichlid (Thorichthys helleri) can move his brood of eggs, attached to a leaf, to a new location if needed.

average, the benefits outweigh the costs. They raise more young this way – and pass on more of their genes to the next generation – than if they did not provide any parental care.

Q: Where do they lay their eggs?

A: Just as with the egg-placing species, the key to a good spawning site is that it should be out of the way of predators. Guarding is much easier if the eggs are in an easily defendable spot, or at least one that offers concealment from predators. Younger fish spawning for the first time, sometimes lay their eggs in poorly chosen places only to see

their efforts at guarding come to nothing as egg-predators clean up – but they soon learn. Some cichlid species cleverly lay their eggs on a detached leaf, allowing them to move their brood to safety if predators threaten or if the water level drops.

Q: How long do single parents guard their eggs?

A: As fry become more mobile and better able to evade predators, parental protection becomes less and less important. At the same time, their guardian must decide whether to continue to care for this batch or start breeding all over again. In doing so, the parent trusts that a majority of the first batch of young will be able to look after themselves. The exact cut-off point depends on all sorts of things, including the stage of the

breeding season and the age of the parent. Also, the larger the brood, the more investment a parent makes in it – fish can count. Many fish, including the spiny eel (*Mastacembelus platysoma*), give up their parental care once the young are large enough to feed independently; in the case of the eel, this is about 30 days after spawning. In addition, there are documented cases of parental fish releasing newly independent fry into areas occupied by large predatory fish. This is because the predator is unlikely to harass tiny fry but will try to eat any of the larger fry predators that approach.

Below: Spiny eels look after their young for an extended period, allowing their offspring to reach independence.

Biparental fish

In a very few species of fish — about 5% of all species — both parents care for the young, sharing the duties of defense and nurturing their offspring. Although this is of enormous benefit to the young, making their chances of survival far higher than would otherwise be the case, it places significant constraints on the parents.

Q: Why is biparental care so unusual in fishes?

A: Although biparental care is undoubtedly good for the offspring, the costs to the parents are high. It may even be said that the needs of the young are in conflict with their parents' needs. If this is the case, why do parental fish do it? Monogamy is rare among fish and occurs only when both parents are needed to defend their breeding territory or feed their young. Without this, the fry would suffer and their chances of reaching adulthood would be slim.

Q: Are both parents equally committed?

A: The battle of the sexes is often keenest in biparental fish.

Female fish have most at stake because it may take some time before they have sufficient reserves to spawn again. In contrast, male parents could desert one brood and quickly father another. Male convict cichlids in Costa Rica do sometimes abandon their partner and young in precisely this way. But the cost to the brood is high — lone females are far less effective at defending the young than if both parents stay to do the job. When abandoned, the female fish sometimes transfer their young to the care of another pair or simply

Below: Together, a pair of wild Amphilophus xiloaensis, *which are endemic to Lake Xiloa, Nicaragua, defend their vulnerable young.*

leave the young themselves in the hope of re-mating with a more trustworthy male.

Q: What stops the male from abandoning the brood?

A: Self-interest is usually at the heart of fish behavior. If a male is to leave his brood, it must be for the likelihood of breeding again, otherwise he would be left with no offspring at all. Studies among biparental fish in the wild have shown that it usually requires two individuals to capture a good territory, so operating alone often just does not work. In addition, the singles market in biparental species is often an unappealing

Cichlid mating games

Males and females each try to produce as many offspring as possible, but that does not mean that they necessarily agree on how this could be achieved.

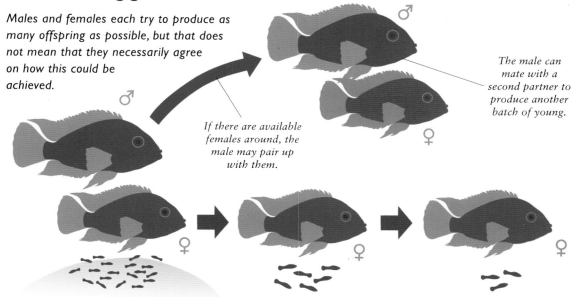

If there are available females around, the male may pair up with them.

The male can mate with a second partner to produce another batch of young.

1 *The pair produce a brood and guard the young before they become free swimming.*

2 *Once the fry are past the early critical stage, the male may desert, leaving the female to guard alone.*

3 *The female, unable to mate again yet, continues to guard a gradually decreasing clutch.*

place and the availability of good mates for abandoning males is often very low. So that they do not put their eggs in the wrong basket, female red devil cichlids have evolved to be able to determine the difference between faithful males and those that are likely to abandon during courtship. With their choices thus restricted, males are often better served by being faithful.

Q: Do fish that guard their young also provide food for them?

A: Some parental species bring food to their young, for example by bringing to the nest decomposing leaves that are rich in infusorians or, in some cases, crushing invertebrates and spitting out particles for the young. Some fish parents go the extra mile and feed their young more directly. Bagrid catfish, for instance, show biparental care and the females

sometimes lay unfertilized eggs as a food source for the young. Discus cichlids are another of a number of species that feed their young directly. Guarding parents produce nutritious mucus on their flanks for the fry to graze on. The mucus provided by the parental fish is higher in essential proteins than in non-breeding fish in their population and supplies the young with a rich food source that significantly enhances their prospects of survival.

Keeping it in the family

The traditional breeding pair arrangement is not for all fish. Some egg-scattering fish spawn in large aggregations, with many males vying for a few females (see page 168). Egg-guarding fish also sometimes spawn in groups – many parents are better than just two. The difference is that with these fish there is a strict hierarchy, very unlike the huge "free-for-alls" of the egg-scatterers. So far, these remarkable groups of communally breeding fish have only been documented in cichlids, among freshwater species, although this breeding pattern is quite widespread throughout Lake Tanganyika.

Q: How is a group of egg-guarding fish composed?

A: In most cases, the group consists of a single large, dominant male with one or more reproductive females. One of the so-called shell-dwelling cichlids, *Lamprologus callipterus*, breeds in large groups, with one male and anything up to 30 females. This species exhibits the greatest known sexual size dimorphism

among vertebrates – males can be anything up to 20 times the weight of the females. Large adult males defend piles of empty snail shells, which they gather or steal from around their territory. The shells are the chosen spawning site of the female *L. callipterus* and once the eggs are laid, the females remain inside the shell for several days, tending the brood, while the male guards his harem. Amongst *Neolamprologus* species, other fish may be resident within the breeding territory. These fish, called "helpers," may number up to 30 per territory and are conspecifics who do not participate in spawning, but do help to guard the territory and

the young of the breeding fish.

Q: How much do the helpers help?

A: Considerably! The more helpers there are, the larger and better the territory the group as a whole can defend. This in turn means that more fry are raised and that the breeding fish, in particular, can take things a little easier, spending more time feeding, for example.

Below: Shell-dwelling cichlids, such as Lamprologus callipterus, *live in harems of 20 or 30 females with a single dominant male.*

Above: Neolamprologus gracilis *lives in family groups where younger generations help to raise successive broods of their siblings.*

Q: Why do the helpers help?

A: There are many reasons why a fish might choose to help out others in their breeding efforts, rather than disperse and set up a territory on its own. To begin with, all the fish in the breeding group benefit from the protection offered by group-living. Studies have shown that fish dispersing to new territories are at a much higher risk of predation than those that stay in one place. As well as this, breeding territories may be few and far between and evidence suggests that by remaining on the territory and assisting with brood care, helpers may eventually get the chance to inherit the territory and become breeders themselves when one of the dominant adults dies. But one of the main reasons for behaving so co-operatively is that helpers are usually tending their own siblings. Helpers have often been born at the nest they now help at, and raising siblings is just as effective an evolutionary strategy as breeding yourself. For example, among *Neolamprologus savoryi* there is only one breeding male, but there may be up to four breeding females on each territory. Each female forms a subgroup within that territory and each has her own specific helpers, usually her own offspring. This makes sense for the helpers, because by assisting their mother rather than other breeding females on the territory, the helpers are caring for their brothers and sisters rather than half-brothers and half-sisters.

Above: For a male Lamprologus ocellatus, *success is defined by the number of shells in his territory. Each may host a breeding female.*

Mouthbrooding in fish

No matter how good the spot that parental fish choose to hide their eggs and young, a certain proportion of the brood – and sometimes all of it – will be lost to predators. In response, certain fish carry their young with them. Some catfish, such as the banjo catfish, carry their young in hollows on the underside of their bodies. Other species have taken things a step further and carry their brood in their mouths. Most predators of eggs and young are no threat to adult fish, so mouthbrooding is an excellent solution to the problem of brood predators.

Q: How widespread is mouthbrooding in fishes?

A: Although by no means common, it is known to occur in five different freshwater fish families. It is a frequent adaptation in Rift Lake cichlids, where high densities of potential predators exist, and also in a number of catfish, the mouthbrooding bettas, including *Betta pugnax* and *B. channoides*, pikeheads, and the arowana. Amazingly, some brood predators have developed

strategies to get at the young, ramming the brooding parent until it surrenders the brood or by fitting their mouth over that of the other fish and sucking out the young.

Q: Which parent mouthbroods the eggs and young?

A: Across the range of mouthbrooding species there are both paternal and maternal mouthbrooders. In the mouthbrooding bettas the male looks after his brood, just as with other species in the genus, such as the Siamese fighting fish. However, whereas

the fighting fish uses bubblenests to protect his young, other bettas mouthbrood them. This is possibly as an adaptation to living in fast-flowing water, where bubblenests would just be washed away. Most cichlids, by contrast, are maternal mouthbrooders, with the exception of the black-chin tilapia (*Sarotherodon melanotheron*). In a few species, including the spatula catfish (*Phyllonemus typus*) and two cichlid genera, both parents brood their young. The

Below: The "egg spots" on the anal fin of male mouthbrooders may help to ensure fertilization of the eggs in females' mouths.

advantage, of course, is that more eggs can be hatched and fry raised if both parents participate; mouthbrooders are severely limited in the numbers of fry they can raise by the size of their buccal cavity. One reason that biparental brooding is so rare is that in maternally brooding species, dominant males can produce more young by breeding with many females, rather than by brooding themselves.

Q: How do the parents brood their young in their mouths?

A: Usually, parental fish take the eggs into their mouths almost immediately after spawning. Many male cichlid mouthbrooders have what are known as egg spots on their anal fins. These spots are thought to mimic eggs, and as a female instinctively moves to gather up these stray eggs, the male can release sperm and fertilize the eggs in the female's mouth. In most other cases, the eggs are laid and fertilized as normal before being gathered into the mouth. Many of these species have larger mouths and distendable throats to accommodate the eggs – you can usually tell when a fish is brooding by the size of its throat. The eggs are circulated by gentle

chewing motions to keep them aerated. Even after they hatch, the young often remain in the mouth, though they are released in order to feed. At the first sign of danger, visual signals from the parent – in some cichlids a head-down posture accompanied by fin flicking – call back the fry. They respond by rushing towards the dark area of their guardian's mouth, which they are hard-wired to recognize. Obviously, while fry are in the mouth it is difficult or even impossible for the parent to feed, although some fish, such as *Tropheus moorii*, manage and, in doing so, provide food for their young.

Above: A pair of Betta channoides *may remain in a spawning embrace for several seconds.*

Above: A male B. channoides *with eggs in his mouth. His devotion is such that he fasts during this time.*

Below: Their mother's mouth remains the safest place for these young Nimbochromis polystigma.

A cuckoo in the nest

Given the costs of rearing young, it is perhaps not surprising that some individuals and even entire species try to side-step the burden and cheat. Of course, the most effective way of avoiding an obligation, is to get someone else to meet it for you and there are several examples of fish doing precisely this.

Q: *Are there any fish that act just like cuckoos?*

A: The cuckoo famously parasitizes songbirds by raiding their nests and discarding an egg contained within while the parents are away for a short period. The cuckoo then lays a replica of the destroyed egg in its place and quickly escapes, leaving the unwitting songbird parents to raise an impostor. Few people realize that many fish species also freeload when it comes to looking after young; indeed, they have adopted an impressive diversity of cunning tactics. One species – the cuckoo catfish (Synodontis multipunctatus) – is perhaps closest in behavior to the eponymous bird. The catfish swim among spawning groups of

mouthbrooding cichlids, eating some of their eggs as they are produced and substituting them with their own. The cichlids then gather the eggs of the trickster and carefully brood them, all the

while apparently unsuspecting. Things get worse for them once these cuckoos hatch because, according to some sources, the young catfish start to make a meal of the cichlid eggs with which they

Cuckoo catfishes

Fish show a wide range of strategies when it comes to producing the next generation, none more remarkable than that of the cuckoo catfish.

1 *Before taking their eggs into the their buccal cavity, mouthbrooders usually spawn on the substrate.*

2 *Spotting a chance, the cuckoo cat dashes in to lay some eggs of its own amid the cichlid's clutch.*

3 *Unawares, the cichlid carefully broods not only its own young but those of the catfish too.*

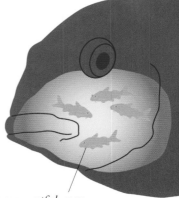

The young catfish may feed on cichlid eggs and fry.

shiners use the chemical cues provided by the sunfish to home in on his territory.

Q: Is it true that some fish guard fry that aren't their own?

A: This happens surprisingly often. A study on convict cichlids in the wild showed that almost half the broods contained adopted youngsters. One reason is that by adopting young, parents dilute the risk of predation to their own offspring. This may be behind the observations made of male midas cichlids invading neighboring territories and kidnapping up to 50 fry to take back to their own broods. As the kidnapped young were not eaten or harassed by their adoptive parents, this behavior is hard to explain. Another study showed that if a female of the biparental mouthbrooder *Perissodus microlepis* was abandoned by her partner and therefore unable to protect her brood effectively, she would gather up her young and deposit them near other brooding pairs close by before fleeing. The new foster families apparently accepted and cared for the new young, raising the possibility that the fish cannot differentiate easily between their own and others' young.

share the buccal cavity. However, the cichlids have a defense mechanism: some species have learned that if they spawn on a sloping surface, the cuckoo catfish cannot parasitize them, possibly because the catfish's eggs roll down the slope.

Q: Do any fish hijack the mating attempts of their conspecifics?

A: Plenty! Small male sunfish (Centrarchidae) pretend to be females to sneak into the defended nests of dominant males and fertilize the eggs laid within. Subordinate male kribs are also known to dash into the midst of things while a dominant pair is breeding and fertilize some eggs before being chased off. But it is not just males that do this. Glass knifefish are weakly electric, using an electric-like radar to find food and conspecifics. Females defend territories among plants,

Above: Both sexes brood the young in Perissodus microlepis, *but if abandoned by her mate, the female may seek alternative childcare arrangements.*

which act as their breeding sites. In an amazing cloak-and-dagger operation, subordinate females switch off their electric organ to prevent detection and sneak into defended territories to shed some of their own eggs while the defender is spawning with a male.

Q: Do any fish use the parental care of other species?

A: Some cyprinids, such as shiners, use a remarkable strategy. Although they are scatter-spawners, they gather to spawn wherever male sunfish build their nests and defend territories. By doing this they can exploit the care that the sunfish provides. The spawning groups of redfin

Livebearing in fish

Laying eggs is a strategy that works well for the majority of fish. Some produce hundreds, even thousands, of eggs in order to try to guarantee that one or two might survive; others lay fewer eggs but invest in placing or caring for them. Another strategy is to skip the egg stage altogether or, more correctly, to allow the eggs to hatch inside their mother and spend these vulnerable few days in the relative safety of her body.

Q: *Which freshwater fish produce live young?*

A: The livebearing species most commonly kept by aquarists all belong to the Poeciliidae, a family that includes the guppies, platies, swordtails, and mollies. But there are other livebearing fish, such as the splitfins, halfbeaks, and limias, as well as some extremely unusual fish, such as the four-eyed fish (*Anableps*) and freshwater stingrays.

Q: *How does it work?*

A: Male livebearers usually have modified anal fins that can be used to transmit tiny packets of sperm to the female. In Poeciliids, this structure is known as a gonopodium. In splitfins and halfbeaks the fin is less highly developed and is known as an andropodium. In either case, fertilization occurs inside the female's body. Once the eggs are fertilized and begin to develop, the mother provides no extra nutrients for the growing young in most cases. Embryonic guppies, platies, mollies, and swordtails feed only on the yolk provided in the egg before fertilization. Splitfin and halfbeak mothers produce eggs with very little yolk but instead provide extra food for their young after fertilization. The embryos obtain their nutrients from their mother via structures

Above: Male guppies constantly seek out females to mate with. In their short lives, wild males may impregnate hundreds of females.

called trophotaeniae, which in some respects are similar to the umbilical cords of mammals. Once the embryos are developed and capable of an independent life, the female gives birth to them, usually one at a time in quick succession.

Q: *How did it all start?*

A: It seems an extraordinary transition for fish to switch from laying eggs to withholding the eggs, using internal fertilization and giving birth to live young. Yet the benefits to these small fishes are clear and there are examples of fish that are intermediate to the egg-laying and livebearing strategies. Killifish species, such as the pearlfish and the swordfin killifish, have structures similar to the gonopodium of male livebearers that may be used in courtship. On the other hand, there is a species among the livebearers, *Tomeurus gracilis*, that lays eggs. Just to show that nothing is ever simple when it comes to the livebearers, there are two species – the Amazon molly (*Poecilia formosa*) and the headwater livebearer (*Poeciliopsis monacha*) – which are all-female. (In fact, the jury is out regarding whether these are actually species in the true sense.) Both mate with males of closely related species and the mating triggers the embryos to start developing, but in the Amazon molly, at least, the sperm does not contribute any DNA and the offspring are all female clones of their mother.

Above: *A guppy gives birth. The young are born one after another and a large female may produce over 100 fry in each batch.*

Below: *Although female guppies invest a great deal in their young, they are not averse to snacking on newborn fry – it's a tough life!*

The life of livebearers

The sudden appearance in the aquarium of tiny fry, exact replicas of their parents, is frequently the first introduction that aquarists have to fish reproduction. As so many species are commonplace and simple to breed, there is sometimes a tendency to consider them as somehow less interesting than other, more testing species. Yet this is to devalue the experience of a truly remarkable group of fish, which have evolved to survive and prosper in extremely testing conditions.

Q: Are livebearing species widespread throughout the world?

A: Yes, they can be found almost everywhere. Livebearers are tremendously successful in their home waters. Their ability to reproduce quickly means that their populations persist even in areas of high predation and their undemanding water requirements, in most cases, allow them to exploit all kinds of habitats. Mosquitofish have been used as agents of biological control in the fight against biting flies and have been spread by man to every continent except Antarctica. Their spread has been so great that in many places they are now considered as pests.

Q: How quickly can livebearers reproduce?

A: Typical Poeciliids, such as the guppy and the swordtail, can reproduce extremely quickly. The females are capable of storing sperm, meaning that they are able to store sperm and use it to fertilize several batches of young in succession. Swordtails can produce eight to ten broods over a period of around eight months after just one mating. Given that in good conditions a large female can produce over 100 fry every 23 to 29 days, this means that a population of just two individuals

Here's one I made earlier

As well as their capacity for maintaining the developing young inside their bodies, female livebearers can also maintain a steady production line of young without remating.

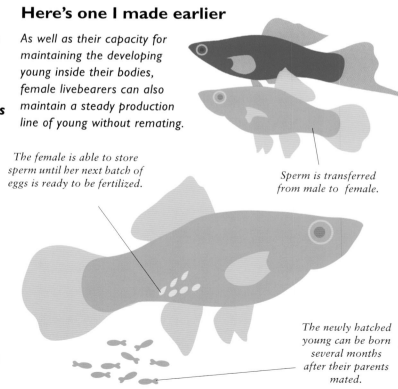

The female is able to store sperm until her next batch of eggs is ready to be fertilized.

Sperm is transferred from male to female.

The newly hatched young can be born several months after their parents mated.

can increase to well over 1,000 inside a year, with only two generations present.

Q: Do all livebearers reproduce this swiftly?

A: No. The number of fry produced by a female is related to her size and age. A swordtail's first brood may number just 20 or so. Only later in life will she be able to produce super batches of over 100. Some species, such as the least killifish (*Heterandria formosa*), produce a steady stream of fry, perhaps one every day, rather than a batch every four weeks or so. To achieve this, the female has to carry a number of different embryos in various stages of maturity, like a fish production line. Livebearer species that are smaller than swordtails produce correspondingly smaller broods, usually of between 20 and 50 fry per brood.

Q: Do livebearers adjust their breeding cycles to match their circumstances?

A: Livebearers produce their largest broods when conditions in their habitat are at their best. At these times the female can garner enough energy to invest in her young and the young

are more likely to prosper with a rich diet after their birth. Furthermore, livebearers such as guppies adjust their breeding patterns according to their habitat. For example, in Trinidad, some guppy populations live with *Rivulus* killifish, which eat juvenile guppies but not adults. The guppies produce larger numbers of offspring and at greater frequency to cope with the heavy burden of fry predation that the killifish place upon the population. Other

Above: In Trinidad's Paria River, newborn guppies suffer heavy predation from Rivulus *killifish. The guppies respond over time by changing their life history.*

guppy populations co-exist with pike cichlids that prey on adults but leave the young guppies alone. These guppies mature sooner – and at a smaller size – and mate earlier in life because their life expectancy as adults is comparatively low.

Chapter 10
Fish in their element

Of the tropical freshwater fish offered for sale, some may have been raised and sold by local hobbyists and certain specialized fish are wild caught. However, the majority are cultivated for the aquarium trade, many of them in the Far East.

For some egglaying species, cultivation means injections with hormones to bring mature adults into breeding condition, at which point they are stripped of eggs or sperm and the young are fertilized and raised in artificial conditions. As well as this, many fish have undergone line-breeding to produce strains of fish very different in appearance from their wild counterparts. They have been selected to exhibit traits that will catch a purchaser's eye, such as long fins or new colors. More recently, hybrid species, such as the parrot cichlid, have been produced under a veil of secrecy regarding their "parental" species. Of course, domestication of animals has been going on throughout human history and, from an aesthetic point of view, whether or not you prefer these varieties is entirely a matter of personal taste. One thing is for certain: breeding fish for the aquarium trade releases the pressure on wild fish populations, which can only be a good thing.

Q: What has a bright domesticated variety of fish got to do with a drab wild fish?

A: Considered across the huge range of fish species available for the home aquarium, relatively few differ greatly in appearance from wild fish. Those species that have been bred to produce different color or fin strains are all entirely natural in the sense that the line-breeders can only work with the materials to hand. For instance, wild-type swordtails are comparatively drab in color, yet generations of selective breeding have produced a dazzling variety of domestic color strains. This would not be possible if the original wild fish did not have the genes for these colors. These genes are rarely expressed in wild fish because they would make the fish stand out and thus a target for predators. However, such

Below: Selectively bred varieties, such as this balloon molly, can be very different from their wild forebears.

constraints do not exist in the aquarium and patient cultivation has brought these characteristics forward. The bottom line is that although brightly colored or long-finned varieties are somewhat unlike their wild forebears in appearance, in genetic terms they are virtually indistinguishable.

Left: A wild male swordtail (Xiphophorus hellerii) has a subtle color pattern of olive-green, with red and green stripes down his flank.

Left: Although this swordtail is only one generation removed from the wild, the influence on its color pattern of domestic breeding is clear to see.

Q: How closely do fish in the home aquarium compare in behavior to their wild counterparts?

A: Domestic fish do not face the day-to-day pressures of their wild counterparts. This makes them less effective at foraging and avoiding predators. This said, the behavior of aquarium fish has been shaped over millions of years of evolution. In comparison, the effects of domestication on aquarium fish behavior over a few, even over hundreds of generations, is relatively subtle. By and large, aquarium fish still show typical wild patterns of schooling behavior,

aggression, territoriality, and activity.

Q: How can studies of wild fish help us to create better conditions for our aquarium fish?

A: Understanding how and why fish behave as they do is a vital part of good fishkeeping. In order to maintain healthy and happy communities of fish in the

Above: Years of selective breeding have produced domesticated fish that are more colorful than their wild forebears. The original color pattern is suffused with orange.

home aquarium, it is important to meet the requirements of the fish in terms of compatibility and conditions, as revealed by studies of wild populations.

New fish in the tank

In the wild, many fish remain in the same locality for most of their lives. During this time, they become familiar with their social and physical environment and with the water chemistry and typical foods. Being moved into a novel habitat, such as a new aquarium, can be extremely traumatic for a fish, causing levels of stress hormones in the bloodstream, such as cortisol, to increase dramatically. If the stress continues over long periods, it can make a fish vulnerable to diseases or may even kill it. By understanding fish behavior, the conscientious aquarist can take steps to minimize the stress to a fish of moving it to a new tank in three vital areas: fish compatibility, tank layout, and water chemistry.

Q: How can I make sure that my new fish is compatible with its tankmates?

A: There are some obvious steps, such as first reading up about the new fish and making sure that it is neither dramatically smaller nor larger than the existing tank inhabitants. Beyond this, it can be important to consider the existing sex ratio in the tank of the species in question and how the new arrivals will affect this. As a general rule, a male-biased sex ratio is bad news for tank harmony. In addition, you should consider the availability of hiding spaces or territories for the new fish. A tank may be huge, yet have limited refuges for a shy fish. The new fish may have to establish a position in the existing pecking order, which may involve a short

Above: Many aquarium fish hail from habitats where there are plenty of hiding places: this mature, planted aquarium provides an excellent home for them.

period of increased aggression, although this should decrease back to normal within 24 hours once the hierarchy is decided. If it does not, then steps may have to be taken to separate warring sides. One way to ensure that a new fish has a more gradual transition is to introduce it at night after feeding the other fish.

Q: How does the tank layout affect a new fish settling in?

A: Fish will rapidly explore a new environment and usually have their new aquarium mapped out within 24 hours, even if this means they investigate under cover of darkness. Whereas most fish use vision to explore, blind cave fish examine new habitats by swimming at increased speed while keeled over at an angle; it seems that they "feel" out their new habitat using their lateral line. Almost without exception, access to plenty of hiding places enables a fish to settle more quickly. Even if it does not use them, a fish feels more secure knowing it has some emergency boltholes. People often opt for a sparse

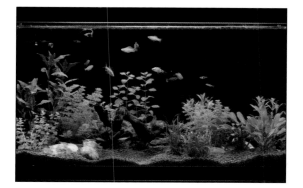

Left: Sensible stocking levels, as seen in this tank, mean that both new arrivals and established inmates are given space to thrive.

layout so that they can see their new purchase, but in the long run the fish will be more relaxed and happy in a more complex, aquascaped habitat and, hopefully, be more visible.

Below: By choosing compatible species, the aquarist can avoid problems caused by excessive aggression in a community tank.

Q: How can I minimize the worst effects of chemical shock?

A: Again, background reading on the water chemistry requirements of a particular species is invaluable. The water in an aquarium can then be tailored to match the needs of its inhabitants in terms of pH, hardness, dissolved oxygen, and temperature. Obviously, part of this is to make sure that the tank inhabitants are matched in terms of their requirements – for example, you should not mix Amazonian catfish with Rift Lake cichlids because each needs dramatically different water chemistry parameters. Finally, do not underestimate the importance of ageing water and treating it to remove chemicals such as chlorine, which are added to make it safe for humans; they can have a serious effect on fish.

Fish behavior and water chemistry

Fish are profoundly affected by the water they live in. Water temperature and chemistry directly affect a fish's physiological processes and in turn influence their behavior.

Q: Why does water chemistry affect fish behavior?

A: The bodies of freshwater fish are full of complex chemicals, including ions and salts. These substances are far more concentrated in the fish's bloodstream than in the water outside and, as a result, water molecules move into the fish by osmosis. To counteract this, the fish must continuously pump water out of their bodies, almost like a leaking ship. They shed this excess water by urinating, while at the same time taking up salts from the water using specialized cells concentrated in the gills. In this way, they are able to maintain their body's chemical balance. If a fish experiences changes in water chemistry, these can throw the physiological balance of their body out of kilter. A sudden change can have serious effects, possibly ending in the death of the animal. But even in normal conditions, this continual chemical balancing act means that fish are acutely sensitive to levels of dissolved substances in their environment.

Q: How does water chemistry affect fish behavior?

A: Fish live with a wide range of different chemicals in their environment, but ammonia is one they particularly respond to. Fish produce ammonia as a by-product of their metabolism, so when they live at high densities, ammonia levels can often be correspondingly high. A study on convict cichlids showed that whereas fish are aggressive at low-ammonia concentrations, an increase in ammonia caused them to decrease their levels of hostility towards one another. Fish tend to fight less when they live in high densities; it is possible to fight a few fish but no individual can take on an army. Therefore, one possible reason for becoming less aggressive as ammonia concentrations increase is that it mimics a rise in the local population. The same effect is

The metabolic balancing act

Like all animals, fish need to balance their body chemistry. Freshwater fish have the particular problem of holding on to vital salts and minerals.

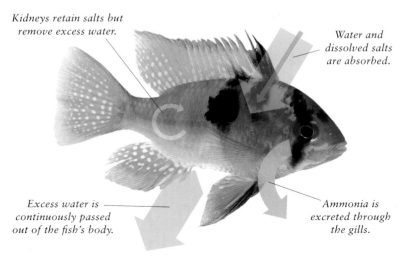

Kidneys retain salts but remove excess water.

Water and dissolved salts are absorbed.

Excess water is continuously passed out of the fish's body.

Ammonia is excreted through the gills.

seen as carbon dioxide levels increase. Again, carbon dioxide is a by-product of fish metabolism and increases when many fish are present. Although kribs fought each other when carbon dioxide levels were low, a small increase in the level of this gas in the water caused them to stop fighting and start schooling.

Q: *Why do fish slow down when it gets colder?*

A: The temperature of fishes' bodies is determined by that of the water. In turn, their metabolic rate, which governs activity levels, is also affected by the water temperature. When guppies are kept at 72°F (22°C), they are much more sluggish and school less effectively, putting them at greater risk of being picked off by

Something in the water

While a high level of ammonia can be toxic to fish, even small changes in background concentrations can have a strong effect on fish behavior.

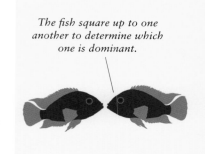

The fish square up to one another to determine which one is dominant.

1 *With low levels of ammonia, aggression is a normal feature of fishes' behavior patterns.*

Below: Water temperature is of critical importance in controling fishes' annual rhythms of breeding and their day-to-day behavior.

2 *High levels of background ammonia suggest there are other fish around and aggression drops.*

an alert predator. As temperatures rise, so does the level of activity of the fish. The number of squabbles between juvenile convict cichlids almost doubles as the temperature increases from 79°F to 86°F (26°C to 30°C). As metabolic rate increases, so too does the need of fish to feed. An increase in temperature from 68°F to 86°F (20°C to 30°C) almost doubles the metabolic rate of many tropical fish, meaning they need correspondingly more food. Aquarists will notice that their fish are far greedier at high temperatures than at low ones.

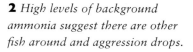

Fish individuals

One facet of behavior that very few people historically expected to see in fish is that of "personality." There seemed little room for such individuality in fish while people still labored under the misapprehension that they had three-second memories and were generally extremely dumb animals.

Q: *So do fish have "personalities"?*

A: Yes! Taking two fish of the same species, you might notice immediately that they are different sexes, or of a slightly different size, or that their color patterns are very slightly dissimilar. Beyond this, the

two fish may well differ in their behavior patterns. Some fish are consistently more aggressive than others, learn more quickly, are more inquisitive, or more likely to come out into the open when others remain hidden. These variations in individual behavior patterns are an entirely natural phenomenon and provide fish with personalities that can be clearly seen in the home aquarium.

Q: *What kinds of*

Right: Behaviorally complex animals, such as this discus cichlid, show distinct personalities and individual differences.

personalities do fish display?

A: One of the main areas of fish personality that has been researched is the willingness of a fish to accept risk. Some individuals seem more or less to ignore things that their tankmates respond to in alarm. Other fish of the same species seem to be extremely timid and take fright at

Left: Despite their sometimes secretive or inactive behavior, many catfish species are amazingly bright.

Above: Fish, such as this jaguar cichlid that provide parental care must have a level of behavioral flexibility and intelligence.

is safe and often remain hidden for much of their lives. They grow more slowly, but once they mature, may fit in several breeding seasons. In some ways, the two strategies are comparable to the fable of the tortoise and hare.

Q: Is the personality of a fish consistent?

A: Although fish do become more cautious in many respects as they age, they do seem to be fairly consistent when facing different contexts. Typically, a "bold" fish will be more aggressive and more of a loner than a shy one. It will explore its environment more quickly than shy conspecifics and out compete them for food, sometimes just by virtue of the way they may be the first to dash into an unknown

the slightest hint of danger. These personality types are referred to respectively as "bold" and "shy." The differences between the two are often not small; in some situations, a shy fish can be over 10 times more risk-averse than bold conspecifics. This is perfectly natural; both strategies can work in the real world. Bold fish seem to use a "live-fast, die-young" strategy. They keep foraging and exploring when others are hiding, with the result that they grow quickly and breed at an earlier age. In the wild, their strategy may mean that they only live for a short period, but if they do reach maturity, they will produce plenty of young because of their size and vigor. Shy fish avoid risk, feeding only when it

situation to grab food.

Q: Are some fish species more likely to display a range of behavior types?

A: Yes. For some species, such as schooling tetras which rely on synchronicity of appearance and behavior, individuality would be clearly disastrous. Other species, such as catfish, cichlids, and gouramis especially, are known to show large variations in "personality" from fish to fish. Wild fish tend to show greater variation because domestic breeding seems to promote boldness, but nonetheless, the fish in an aquarium are individuals.

Below: In schooling fish, expressing individual differences in behavior is potentially disastrous.

Fish behaving badly

Even when provided with what appears to be the most naturalistic conditions, fish sometimes behave strangely or uncharacteristically in the home aquarium. Aquarists may face a variety of bugbears, but the following questions are some of the most common.

Q: My group of tetras schooled beautifully at first, but now they're spread out across the aquarium. Why is this?

A: Because schooling is primarily thought to be an anti-predator response, the school acts as a refuge for fish when they are stressed. As your fish have acclimatized to their new surroundings, they have become more relaxed and ceased to school quite so tightly. Congratulations – you have relaxed and happy fish!

Q: One fish in my tank makes life a misery for all the others. Why is it doing this and how can I stop it?

A: If a fish is dominant to its tankmates, or claims the tank as its territory, things can get tricky for the other aquarium inhabitants. Most home

Above: Fish in a retailer's tank can often show very different behavior patterns to those that they display when they have settled into the home aquarium.

aquariums are smaller than the typical territory of a fish, so if one individual decides to be boss, all its tankmates may suffer. In the confines of the aquarium, the other fish cannot escape as they would in the wild. Their continued presence in the area may hence be interpreted by the dominant fish as a challenge. This situation can be an extremely difficult to resolve and in some instances may only be tackled by separating the fish. As with all these things, prevention is better than cure, so research is essential before stocking a tank to ensure compatibility. Also bear in mind that fish are more likely to

Below: These cardinal tetras are spread out over the entire length of this lavishly planted tank. They are not tightly schooling because they are happy and relaxed!

tolerate heterospecifics (different species) over conspecifics, and females over males, so ensure that the sex ratio is biased towards females if possible. Sometimes aggression can be dispersed by adding more fish, since there is a limit to how many fish a bully can chase. This is why densely populated Lake Malawi cichlid communities work, but it depends very much on the species in question.

Q: *How can I encourage a shy fish to come out?*

A: It can be extremely frustrating to lay out money for a fabulous fish specimen, only for it then to lurk unseen in various refuges. There are many possible causes of this secretive behavior. The fish may be nocturnal, or a member of a typically shy and retiring species, such as a kuhli loach. It may be difficult to find a solution and you will have to content yourself with occasional glimpses. Alternatively, the fish may be stressed in its environment. Getting it to relax is all about making it feel secure, so provide plenty of hiding places. Consider using so-called dither fish; for instance, a school of tetras milling around in the tank may help to convince the hider that it is safe to come out. You should also determine whether the fish is in poor health or being harassed by the other tankmates, in which case separate it for a period to build it back up.

Below: Fish often seek refuge in a strange situation. In most cases, the answer is to be patient. When the fish grow more comfortable, they will emerge.

Above: Fairly high population levels in Lake Malawi cichlid aquariums such as this can help to dilute aggression between the fish.

Q: *I bought a new fish, but even though I thought all the tank covers were tight it managed to jump out overnight. Why?*

A: The shock of moving into a new environment is thought to trigger this jumping behavior. Aquatic animals are far more at risk than terrestrial ones because their body chemistry is so closely linked to that of the water. Even with a cautious transition, new fish may jump on their first night, having spent the first day perhaps either hiding or moving about fretfully. The answer is to plug all the gaps in the covers and to keep the tank covered, especially at night and during rapid changes in atmospheric pressure, for example during storms.

Fish breeding badly

If fish reproduction is complex in the natural world, it can seem doubly so in the home aquarium. Sometimes it can be the refusal of fish to breed that perplexes the aquarist, at other times it may be some apparently strange behavior during a breeding cycle that causes the problem. From the sudden appearance of a brood of unexpected livebearer fry to the pairing and subsequent aggression of some hitherto inoffensive dwarf cichlids, when fish start to experience urges it can turn a balanced aquarium community upside-down overnight.

Q: I've tried everything but my fish won't breed. What am I doing wrong?

A: Assuming the basics – that you have at least a male and a female and have provided the appropriate conditions in terms of water chemistry, temperature, and a dedicated breeding tank – it can be extremely frustrating to see all your efforts apparently come to nothing. But one simple extra step may be all that is required for success. Sometimes, fish respond to a particular trigger,

such as a drop in temperature to imitate the onset of spring rains. This can be especially effective if it accompanies a low-pressure weather system – even fish in an aquarium will be aware of this. For other species, high temperatures combined with plenty of live food (a good idea) and a spawning site they approve of, be it a clump of plants or rocks, may do the trick. There is no substitute for careful research.

Taking charge of the tank

Fish territories in the wild are often considerably larger than the average tank. Little wonder then that if a pair sets up home, chaos can follow.

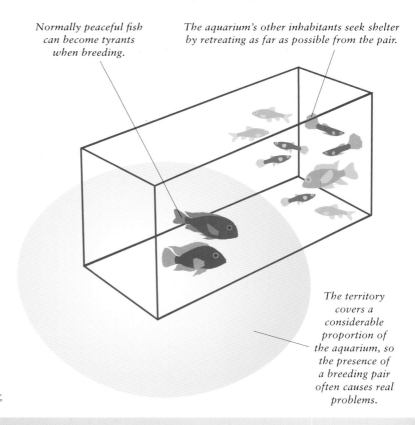

Normally peaceful fish can become tyrants when breeding.

The aquarium's other inhabitants seek shelter by retreating as far as possible from the pair.

The territory covers a considerable proportion of the aquarium, so the presence of a breeding pair often causes real problems.

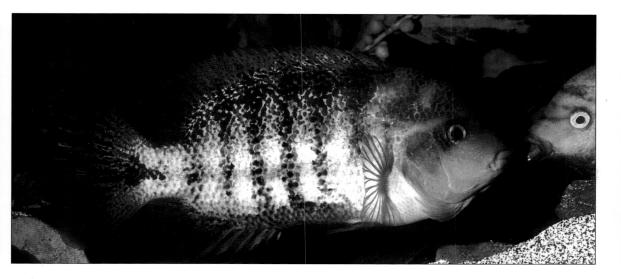

Above: Fish that breed in a community aquarium, especially territorial cichlids, can cause disruption for all the other fish.

Q: My fish won't stop breeding and it's creating havoc. What can I do?

A: If the fish have decided that they want to breed, there is little you can do about it. In fact, it is a testament to your skills as an aquarist that the fish are breeding. But when a pair of territorial fish decide they want to annex a large part of the community aquarium, it is extremely disruptive to the other inhabitants. There the options are limited; either move one or both of the breeding pair into a new aquarium or put up with it.

Q: My fish are breeding but with the wrong species. How can I put this right?

A: In some fish the urge to breed is so strong that if they lack an appropriate partner they may spawn with a closely related species, or in the case of some cichlids, two females may spawn together. Although hybrids are often infertile, this is not always the case and it is clearly important not to blur the gene pool of two separate species by putting hybrids on the market. If a pair of fish of different species breed, consider adding the right partners or separating them. As for the offspring, by all means look after them but do not sell them to the local aquarium shop.

Q: My fish are breeding, but they eat their own young. Why do they do this and how can I stop it?

A: Species that do not care for their young often eat their own eggs and fry. But it seems strange to see parents who have cared for their young for days suddenly turn on them and eat them. In the wild, the parents would drive off their young or abandon them. Their parental instinct is "switched off" once they are ready to breed again. In the aquarium, there is no place for the young to disperse to and the change in their parents' priorities spells death for the young. The safest solution is to separate the young from their parents once they become free swimming.

Index

Credits

The publishers would like to thank the following photographers for providing images, credited here by page number and position: (B) Bottom, (T) Top, (C) Center, (BL) Bottom left, etc.

Aqua Press (M-P and C Piednoir): 42, 49, 65(B), 66, 79(T), 99(T), 161(B), 168, 170, 174(B), 186, 187(T,B)

David Baines (University of Leicester) 75 (TL)

Dave Bevan: 81, 115

Marc Botham: 90(C), 124, 189

Ian Fuller: 176

Zhou Hang: 141(BR), 183(T,C)

Neil Hepworth: 60(TR), 153(B), 174(T), 193(T)

Ad Konings: 10(C,B), 13(T), 29(T), 39, 40(T), 44, 51(T), 53(B), 54, 59(T), 65(T), 67(T), 69(B), 70(C), 72, 73(T,B), 83(T,B), 88, 93(T), 97(B), 99(B), 100, 101(T,B), 120, 122, 126, 136, 145(T,B), 146, 147(B), 148, 149(T). 152, 155(B), 159(B), 177(T,B), 178, 180, 181(T), 183(B), 185, 191(T)

Jan-Eric Larsson-Rubenowitz: 103(T)

Oliver Lucanus: 84(B), 89, 162, 164, 201

Microscope and Graphic Imaging Center © 1997, 1998 California State University, Hayward: 69 (TL)

Arend van den Nieuwenhuizen: 173, 175

Peter Riley 60(B)

Geoff Rogers © Interpet Publishing Ltd: *Half-title, Full title, Copyright/Contents*, 6, 8(T), 11, 12, 13(B), 15, 18, 19, 20, 21, 22, 26, 27, 28, 30, 31, 32, 33, 34, 35, 36, 37, 38, 40(B), 43, 45, 46, 47, 51(B), 53(T), 58, 59(B), 67(B), 68, 70(T), 71, 75(B), 76, 77, 78, 79(B), 85(B), 86, 91, 93(B), 94, 95, 96, 97(T), 104, 106(T), 107, 108, 109, 112, 113, 116, 117, 119, 125, 128, 129, 130, 131, 133, 134, 138, 140, 141(T), 142, 143, 144, 150, 151, 153(T), 154, 155(T), 156, 157, 158, 159(T), 161(T), 165, 166(TL), 169, 181(B), 182, 190, 191(C,B), 192, 193(B), 195, 196, 197, 198, 199

Sue Scott: 57, 123(T,B)

Rowena Spence (University of Leicester): 14

Iggy Tavares: 8(B), 9, 63(T), 64, 87, 147(T), 149(B), William A. Tomey: 17 (T,C,B), 60(C), 63(B), 80, 82, 85(T), 90(B), 103(B), 167

Kevin Webb: 84(T), 106(C), 166(C)

The computer graphics on the pages shown have been based on the following sources:

Page 19 : *Fish and Their Behavior* by G.K.H. Zupanc 2nd edition, Tetra-Press, Melle (1988).

Page 36: *Fish Behavior in the Aquarium and in the Wild* by Stephan Reebs, Comstock/Cornell Paperbacks, Cornell University Press (page 129).

Page 62 and 63: Haffter, P. *et al.* 1996. The identification of genes with unique and essential functions in the development of the zebrafish, *Danio rerio*. Development 123: 1-36.

Page 74-5: *Vertebrate Life* by F. Harvey Pough, Christine M. Janis and John B. Heiser, published by Prentice-Hall Inc., New Jersey, 1999 (page 235). Modified from K.F. Liem in A.G. Kluge et al., 1977, *Chordate Structure and Function,* 2nd edition, Macmillan, New York, NY.

Page 80: *The Vertebrate Eye* by G.L. Walls, published by Hafner, New York, 1963.

Page 86: *The Teeth of Plecostomus, an Armored Catfish,* Theodore H. Eaton Jnr., *Copeia*, Vol. 1935, No. 4 (December 31, 1935), pp. 161-163.

Author's acknowledgements

Thanks to my wonderful wife, Alison, for her help with this book and her patience. Thanks to my parents, Barbara and Gerald, for everything. Finally, thanks also to Matt and the staff at Ocean Commotion, Clarendon Park Road, Leicester, for their advice and assistance.

Publisher's acknowledgements

The publishers would like to thank the following for their help in providing facilities for photography: Amwell Aquatics, Soham, Cambridgeshire. Aquatic Warehouse, Enfield, Middlesex. BAS, Bolton, Lancashire. Betta Aquatics, Elmstead Market, Essex. Kesgrave Tropicals, Ipswich, Suffolk. Adrian Burge, British Killifish Association. Catfish Study Group (UK). Keith Cocker, Norwich and District Aquarist Society. Ely Aquatic Center, Ely, Cambridgeshire. Hertfordshire Fisheries, St. Albans, Hertfordshire. Kesgrave Tropicals, Ipswich, Suffolk. Maidenhead Aquatics, Crowland, Lincolnshire. Maidenhead Aquatics, St. Albans, Hertfordshire. Maidenhead Aquatics, East Grinstead, Surrey. Pets at Home, Ipswich, Suffolk. Pier Aquatics, Wigan, Lancashire. Colin and Kay Sargeant, Stowmarket, Suffolk. Shirley Aquatics, Solihull, Warwickshire. Shotgate Aquatics, Billericay, Essex. Swallow Aquatics, Aldham, Colchester, Essex. Swallow Aquatics, East Harling, Norfolk. Swallow Aquatics, Rayleigh, Essex. Swallow Aquatics, Southfleet, Kent. Dr. Ashley Ward, University of Leicester. Wharf Aquatics, Pinxton, Nottinghamshire. Wholesale Tropicals, Bethnal Green, London. Wildwoods Water Gardens, Enfield, Middlesex.

Publisher's note